THE WORLD
TO COME

THE WORLD TO COME

A PORTAL TO
HEAVEN ON EARTH

DEREK LEMAN

Unless otherwise noted, Scripture quotations are taken from:

Complete Jewish Bible © 1998 by David H. Stern,
Published by Jewish New Testament Publications, Inc.

Cover Design by
Josh Huhn, Design Point, Inc.
Layout Design by
Valerie Levy, Drawing Board Studios

12 11 10 09 08   5 4 3 2 1

ISBN 13: 978-1-880226-04-9
ISBN 10: 1-880226-04-9

Library of Congress Control Number: 2008923014
Printed in the United States of America

Lederer Books
A division of
Messianic Jewish Publishers
6120 Day Long Lane
Clarksville, MD 21029

Distributed by
Messianic Jewish Resources International
Order Line: (800) 410-7367
E-mail: lederer@messianicjewish.net
Website: www.messianicjewish.net

I dedicate this book to my wife, Linda, and our eight children.
I experience a bit of the World to Come every day with them.
I know that love endures and because of Linda
I have tasted already of that enduring love.
The joy that we have together in our children helps me
completely reevaluate the expectations of life our society
promotes as true happiness. I have truly found in them some hint
of the greater joy of relationship.
Linda, Deborah, Nathanael, Rachel, Hannah, Josiah, Samuel, Miriam,
and our newest child, David, thank you for all the good times.

Derek

Other books by author:

Proverbial Wisdom & Common Sense
A Messianic Jewish Approach to Today's Issues from the Proverbs
© 1999 Messianic Jewish Publishers

Jesus Didn't Have Blue Eyes
Reclaiming Our Jewish Messiah
© 2004 Mt. Olive Press

Paul Didn't Eat Pork
Reappraising Paul the Pharisee
© 2005 Mt. Olive Press

A New Look at the Old Testament
© 2007 Mt. Olive Press

CONTENTS

INTRODUCTION

I wasn't raised in a religious home, so my earliest thoughts about the afterlife came from cartoons like *Tom and Jerry*. Whenever a character died, they became transparent, grew wings, found themselves in a white robe, and ascended into heaven. Heaven, apparently, was a purely spiritual or non-material place. Cartoons can be surprisingly influential in a person's worldview. Although I considered myself an atheist as a young adult, I defaulted at times to my earlier view of the afterlife. I wanted to believe in something.

Most people believe that death is not the end. The hope that death is not the end is too important for most people to dismiss. It is not common to find someone who will baldly assert that death leads only to non-existence.

Yet there are voices opposed to the idea of the hereafter and occasionally they even belong to religious leaders. A friend was shocked when attending a liberal Jewish funeral where the rabbi implied that we live on only in the memory of loved ones. Where was the powerful Jewish hope, "All Israel has a share in the World to Come"?[1]

Then there is the perspective of famed atheist Isaac Asimov:

I don't believe in an afterlife, so I don't have to spend my whole life fearing hell, or fearing heaven even more. For whatever the tortures of hell, I think the boredom of heaven would be even worse.[2]

In some deep place, I think many people fear that the afterlife will be boring. The *Tom and Jerry* version of heaven, floating on the clouds in a white robe, is an uninspiring vision to be sure. Who wants to spend eternity as a ghost with angel's wings?

In fact, that *Tom and Jerry* heaven is more than just an idea in a cartoon. Certain very real philosophical ideas stand behind a view of the afterlife as ghostly and non-material. Are material things some-how unspiritual and unworthy of eternal existence? Is the body a prison for the soul? If our view of the afterlife is non-material, then we will look at material things in this world as less important than the "spiritual." Ideas about the afterlife have relevance for living life in the present.

What is the World to Come? Why does Jewish tradition use this term for the afterlife? Why not talk about going to heaven or to the great beyond? Many and varied views of the afterlife present themselves to us.

Sometimes people are afraid to talk about the World to Come, as if it is impossible to really know much about it. Randy Alcorn, in his book *Heaven*, mentions a common objection people have with regard to studying the afterlife: "No eye has seen, no ear has heard and no one's heart has imagined all the things that God has pre-pared for those who love him."[3] Yes, says Alcorn, but how many read the next verse, "It is to us, however, that God has revealed these things"?[4]

If it is true, and I think it is, that our belief about the afterlife af-fects our view of this present life, then the study of it is all the more important. The subject of the World to Come deserves neither a yawn nor a skeptical smirk. Contrary to such cynicism, the book of Hebrews attributes Abraham's faithfulness to a clear vision: "For he looked forward to the city which has foundations, whose builder and maker is God."[5]

The familiar line about being too heavenly minded to be any earthly good has it exactly backwards. Most of us are not heavenly minded enough and so we are too little earthly good. The diminishing conversation about the hereafter in some religious communities is not a positive sign. It needs to be reversed. As A. J. Conyers puts it:

Even to one without religious commitment and theological convictions, it should be an unsettling thought that this world is attempting to chart its way through some of the most perilous waters in history, having now decided to ignore what was for nearly two millennia its fixed point of reference—its North Star. The certainty of judgment, the longing for heaven, the dread of hell . . .[6]

A healthy fear of judgment restrains evil decisions, causing people to think about the greater consequences of their actions. Should world leaders be making decisions that mean life or death to thousands or even millions without a firm belief in the life to come and the certainty of judgment? A belief in and longing for reward in the life to come motivates us to make selfless choices to do good in this world. Should we be living our lives largely in ignorance of the hereafter?

The fact is, the hope of future paradise is vital to the full experience of this present life. Abraham was faithful through many years without even seeing the birth of an heir. He kept following God against all evidence. He was carried by his certainty that the promises of God would be fulfilled in a future age. And Yeshua commended such thinking to us as well in Matthew 6:19. He called us to a forward-looking lifestyle, a way of storing up treasure in heaven.

Of course, objections to discussing what the World to Come will be like come from many places. Some followers of Yeshua are convinced that the afterlife is an impenetrable mystery. Many non-religious people would suggest a similar objection. How can we know anything about the afterlife at all? Who has been there and back and can reliably tell us? Indeed, it is faith on two points that can give us a reason for the hope of future life: the fact that God has truly spoken in the scriptures of Judaism and Christianity and the certainty that one man, the central man in God's redeeming plan, has gone beyond and returned.

The rabbis were not afraid to talk about the World to Come. The Mishnah and Talmud have many sayings about it. They were persuaded that Isaiah and other prophets provided a true vision of things to come. Neither have the great leaders of Christendom been afraid to speak about it. They were persuaded that Yeshua the Nazarene died and was resurrected.

So we will explore the nature of the World to Come. We will look for answers to important questions. What will it be like for those who enter the World to Come? What will it be like for those who do not? What events will lead up to the World to Come? What are the visions of different prophets and apostles who wrote on these matters? What hope does the World to Come bring to this present world?

Certain misconceptions will be challenged. Certain views of the World to Come are too limited. Others are simply wrong. Studying this vital subject, it is a good idea to be open to new paradigms that are supported by scripture.

I write this book as a member of the Messianic Jewish community. We are Jews and non-Jews living our lives in a Jewish manner under the teaching of our Messiah and rabbi, Jesus. We think Jesus would be quite at home in our Sabbath services and with our communal prayers.

You will find some Messianic Jewish terminology in this book. We prefer to call the Messiah "Yeshua," his Hebrew name, though we are not averse to calling him Jesus. We want all to understand that Jesus is Lord for us and will one day be so for all Israel and the nations.

We prefer to say Adonai or HaShem in place of God's name. The custom in Christianity is to say "the LORD." Adonai is simply a Hebrew expression more familiar to Jews. Adonai is pronounced Ah-doe-NIGH and essentially means LORD. HaShem means "the Name," and is a way of avoiding using his holy name in a casual manner.

I talk about "the Torah" in this book, a term that has different meanings in different contexts. Usually I use Torah in its simplest sense: the writings of Moses and God's commands to Israel.

Those of us in the Messianic Jewish community see many promises yet to be fulfilled. We do not assume that the great promises of the days of Messiah and the World to Come were conditional upon Israel's obedience to the covenant. We do not envision a shift from Israel to the Church in God's promises. We take seriously the continuing role of Israel as the spearhead of God's redemption of this world very seriously.

We will explore the World to Come as those who look forward to roaming its everlasting hills. We begin with "Magic and Desire," a foreshadowing of the nature of life in the World to Come. From there we move to "The Vision of the Prophets," a presentation of the glories of the future age as recorded by Israel's prophets.

After this journey into imagination, we build a foundation of vital theology about Israel and the nations in chapters 3 and 4. Israel's role is not incidental, so we consider "Israel as the Vessel" in chapter 3, introducing the idea from scripture that God redeems the world through Israel. Chapter 4, "The Nations as the Goal," develops the way God's redemption spreads from Israel to the ends of the earth.

Chapters 5 and 6 bring to bear some key New Testament information about the World to Come and the events leading up to it. Yeshua's kingdom preaching must shape our awareness of the World to Come and how we are to prepare for it. John's vision in Revelation is clearly indispensable for understanding our future hope. I argue that John maintained the Jewish expectation but wrote the nations more into the story, giving a fuller picture in some ways than Israel's prophets.

"Hints of Heaven" (chapter 7) is a different sort of exploration. I propose that the joys and desires of this present world give us insight into the nature of the World to Come. "Horrors of Hell" (chapter 8) is an attempt to understand the judgment side of the World to Come without overstating what the Bible really says.

Chapters 9 and 10 draw us into the subject of events leading up to the World to Come. "The Drama of the Coming Ages" (chapter 9) traces the journey through future stages of history. Then "The Days of Messiah" (chapter 10) focuses on the earthly reign of Messiah, which precedes the Final Age, the New Earth. I interpret Revelation's thousand-year kingdom as literal and see the days of Messiah as a transition into the Final Age.

The next two chapters flow out of the question: What is the greatest thing in the World to Come? "Love" (chapter 11) is about the quality that brought the world into being and will endure forever. Love is the greatest value and all love practiced here will matter there. "The Holy One" (chapter 12) is about the central joy of the World to Come, being drawn ever nearer to God who waits for us.

Finally, in "Further Up and Further In" (chapter 13), we consider an image from C. S. Lewis's imaginative book *The Great Divorce*. It is possible, I suggest, that we do not receive all knowledge at the beginning of the World to Come. It may be a quest for ever-increasing joy. I can think of no journey or joy or satisfaction I'd rather experience.

Two appendices are included. The first should be valuable to anyone who desires to study the Bible's teaching on final things: a list of scriptures about the World to Come. The second appendix summarizes the ages of history and the future, explaining some theological themes from each.

Finally, what do you do with the kind of information you will find in this book? Information is good, but transformation is better. My hope is that somehow I will spark your imagination about the wonders of the World to Come. This is not idle future speculation. A clear vision of God's promise is mandatory for God's people in this present world. After all, we are called to join with God in redeeming and transforming this world into the World to Come. Eternal life does not begin at death or at the end of the Age. It begins now. And the giver of this life has work for us to do. He always uses his creatures. In that sense, the World to Come is already (but not yet) here.

CHAPTER 1

Magic and Desire

I mainly remember two things from my high school reading of *Moby Dick*. I remember the end and beginning. The end, of course, is one of the great scenes of fiction, as the defiant Ahab spits on the great white whale while sinking to his doom. But there is something even more evocative about the beginning. Melville engages in a discourse about desire, specifically the desire of mankind to be near bodies of water. It is one of the peculiarities of human nature I had never considered.

Ishmael travels to a seaside town, bent on signing himself onto a whaling ship. It is a Sunday in quaint New England and the town is full of Sunday Sabbath picnickers. Ishmael muses on what draws them, "Are the green fields gone? What do they here?"

The more he walks along the streets the more masses he sees "fixed in ocean reveries." It seems that people need to go to the "extremest limit of the land," not choosing to picnic in the shade of warehouses. They need to get as close as possible to water without falling in. Ishmael asks, "Does the magnetic virtue of the needles of the compasses of all those ships draw them thither?"

As he ponders this beach behavior, he realizes this human fascination includes more than just the ocean:

Say you are in the country, in some high land of lakes. Take almost any path you please, and ten to one it carries you down into a dale, and leaves you there by a pool in the stream. There is magic in it. Let the most absent-minded of men be plunged in his deepest reveries—stand that man on his legs, set his feet a-going, and he will infallibly lead you to water, if water there be at all in that region.

Even artists, he notes, invariably place a stream or pond in their romantic landscapes. There is a human, uncontrollable desire to see water in a natural setting. It is to see the placid, mirror-like surface or the rolling waves or the tumbling currents and eddies by which we are captivated with an almost animal nature.

What is behind this desire for streams, placid ponds, and boundless oceans? Is there anything like that desire for other parts of this world and this life? I would have to say yes. Inexplicable desire is not limited to bodies of water. Other things call to us as well.

I recently climbed to a place about 10,000 feet up in the Rockies. It was bitter cold, not because the temperature was so low, but because I was underdressed and my feet were wet from walking in knee-deep snow. I was with two companions, men I barely knew. We weren't sure we could find what we were looking for, a trout pond on a plateau in the mountain.

We experienced a number of things that would have set us back down the mountain to our warm, dry cabin. There was a little fear when we found cougar tracks. There was exhaustion as none of us were used to the lack of oxygen at that altitude. There was pain as our feet became numb with cold and were becoming blistered. There was misgiving as the snow covered the trail and we could not be certain we were going the right direction.

Yet we kept going. What was the desire that drew us? It wasn't hunger. We planned to throw back the small, wild brook trout we hoped to catch. It wasn't scientific study or a journalistic impulse to photograph the small lake and the mountain peak mirrored behind it. There was no profit in our venture. No, we were drawn by adventure and desire.

Our hike of more than an hour was rewarded when we guessed that a certain ridge might be hiding our trout pond. As we got closer, we saw mist rising above the ridge—water! Ascending over that last ridge is a moment I will remember if I live into my nineties. We topped the hill and there it was—a scene fit for a painting. A meadow skirted a shallow, clear lake and behind it the snow-covered peak of the mountain extended up another few thousand feet. We found our Shangri-La.

Desire. I associate it strongly with a dark, romantic wood. I cannot deny the attraction of wild water. Many have fallen to the temptation to tackle a mountain climb. We love our luxury but for recreation we give all that up for a rugged hike, armed only with a backpack, water bottle, and walking stick. We are drawn to trees, rivers, and mountains.

My life was greatly changed by the landscapes of Narnia and Middle Earth. Millions of other Lewis and Tolkien fans also fell in love with those magic places. Perhaps it was something different for you, a Disney landscape painted with beauty in Snow White or a painting or a picture in a children's book or a little section of woods by your house. You've most likely felt it too.

These longings, these desires, are not animal. We are not drawn to streams by thirst or to meadows by hunger. The longing is spiritual. It is an inner call for heaven, the World to Come, the better world we know inside will exist in the hereafter.

SHEEP, MEADOWS, AND THE MESSIAH

As we sit in our plastic chairs, typing plastic keys and reading plastic screens, there is still a little of the nature-lover in all of us. Rolling hills, wild grass, fluffy white sheep dotting the landscape—they seem a better way of life sometimes when we grow tired of the recirculated air. We could picture ourselves, sitting on a sunny hilltop, looking over our flock with a staff in hand.

Of course, in our imagination or in a painting of a pastoral scene, we romanticize the experience. In real life, most of us would be put off by the heat, the bugs, and the smell of real animals, longing for an air-conditioned office even if we are tired of plastic. Yet, what if? What if growing fantastic gardens and tending sheep were not so unpleasant? What if there was a place where the world worked with us instead of against us?

Do we really think our lives are completely better for all our technological existence? Do the joys of television, internet, and high-tech mattresses really make up for what we have lost? I'm not overlooking the vast improvement in medicine. It is a wonderful thing that most mothers survive childbirth and we have Novocain to make a tooth extraction a little easier.

I mean, has our sense of wonder improved? For all our fancy ways, we still pay out our entertainment money to see adventure, romance, and documentaries about nature. Now we see nature on a plastic screen instead of in person. Now we get our stories, and far too many of them so we cannot remember them all, with sound and visual effects.

Even our sense of time is diminished. We are in a hurry. Is a movie longer than two hours? Who can sit still that long? Give us a short list of facts and don't bore us in magazine and newspapers. Who wants to sit down and read a newspaper or magazine when we can sample a little here and there all over the world on a dozen websites in five minutes? Who has time to read a poem, seriously, when we have so many opportunities for amusement and mindless fact gathering?

It may seem odd to some that the Jewish-prophetic vision of the hereafter is pastoral and agricultural. The prophets spoke of reaping the fruit before the sowing was finished and of a vine and fig tree for every person. Immediately some object, "That was all they knew; they envisioned something that made sense in their limited world." Never mind the immediate reply—our sterile existence is all we know and we imagine what makes sense in our limited world.

Will asphalt really add something to the World to Come? Do you imagine we can live without paving over paradise after Messiah comes? Will we need laptops and MP3 players? If everyone had more time for art and music, couldn't we just hear them live and not on a recording of a recording heard on speakers that almost get the sound right?

No matter what world we live in, pastoral or plastic, there is something unfulfilled. Maybe it is separation from the beauty of creation or maybe it is disillusionment with the brokenness of creation. Pick your poison.

Yet Moses and the Jewish prophets showed us a better future. The Jewish apostles added to the picture. Over the years many themes in Judaism and Christianity have confused the picture. Different philosophers and religious thinkers have painted different pictures, all too dull to be God's perfect world. Views of the World to Come as diverse as white sheets, clouds, and harps on the one hand or a Torah Study hall full of men debating the details of ancient scriptures on the other, distort the true grandeur that awaits. Morbid Hades and ethereal Isles of the Blessed also fall short of God's glorious New Earth. Mythology and philosophy need to be replaced in our thinking by the vision of Israel's prophets, a vision of tangible paradise.

WITLESS SHADOWS IN A MURKY WORLD

N. T. Wright described one of the world's earliest views of the hereafter as a world of witless shadows. He was describing the view of the Sumerians, Mesopotamians, Egyptians, and Greeks.[7] This ancient view of life after death is found in the Greek Hades, the Hall of the Dead. Hades is not a synonym for hell, but a holding place, and in classic literature, everyone goes there.

In Mesopotamian literature, it shows up in funerary inscriptions about the ghosts of the dead requiring offerings to feed them.[8] In Egypt it shows up in the custom of burying the dead with their needed possessions and in the myths of Osiris, god of the underworld.[9] Surprisingly, this was still the view of the Greeks at the time of Homer. Wright helps readers vividly picture this dismal view of the life to come with a famous scene from *The Iliad*:

> There came to him the hapless spirit of Patroclus, in all things like his very self, in stature, in fair eyes and in voice, and in raiment was he clad withal; and he stood above Achilles' head and spoke to him, saying: "Thou sleepest, and hast forgotten me, Achilles. Not in my life was thou unmindful of me, but now in my death! Bury me with all speed that I pass within the gates of Hades. Afar do the spirits keep me aloof, the phantoms of men that have done with the toils, neither suffer they me to join myself to them beyond the River, but vainly do I wander the wide-gated house of Hades. And give me thy hand, I pitifully entreat thee, for never more again shall I come back from out of the land of Hades.". . .Achilles held out his arms to clasp the spirit, but in vain. It vanished like a wisp of smoke and went gibbering underground. . . . [He said] "Ah, then it is true that something of us does survive, even in the halls of Hades, but with no intellect at all, only the ghost and semblance of a man."[10]

Patroclus was a shade, a witless shadow from Hades. And that was the fate of a hero! This view of the hereafter included some sense of intellect and awareness of the World to Come, but far less than we enjoy now. There would be no physical existence there and only a little spiritual existence if any at all.

It was Plato who advanced a brighter view of the hereafter and the Platonic view has affected some Christian and Jewish versions of the hereafter ever since. For Plato, the body was a prison for the soul.[11] The immaterial soul was far better, the essence of our being, just as a tree has an essence that it shares in common with all trees and a raindrop with all raindrops, not matter how different they are. And death was not a ticket to one place, a one-size-fits-all itinerary. Those who merited it would go to the Isles of the Blessed and those who did not to Tartarus.[12] The hereafter could be a happy place or an unending torment. The hereafter was not physical, but spiritual. The physical plane would be transcended and the spiritual was better. The hereafter was discontinuous with the here and now. Plato also envisioned another view, very similar to Eastern religious concepts: reincarnation or the transmigration of the soul.[13]

The Jewish prophets and apostles envisioned something very different. The things created by God are good. Trees, rivers, and mountains are not to be left behind. The prophetic vision of the World to Come is a lot like this one, only better. It is a world as God meant this one to be. It is the world we desire inside, the world we catch glimpses of in imagination and poetry and art.

MAGIC HILLS

"The desire of the righteous will be granted," says Solomon, and "the desire of the righteous ends only in good."[14] "I will restore Israel to his pasture, and he shall feed on Carmel and in Bashan, and his desire shall be satisfied on the hills of Ephraim and in Gilead." [, says Adonai].[15] "Delight yourself in [Adonai] and he will give you the desires of your heart," the Psalmist encourages us.[16]

There is something about desire that leads either to heaven or hell. We know the difference. Many of the things we truly desire are heavenly, even if we only see them in misshapen and inferior forms. Love, laughter, light, and loveliness will dwell in the World to

Come. Unspoiled pleasure will be there. In the here and now we get glimpses.

We pass a small wood left standing in suburbia or we come upon a stream and we get a sighting of it. We hear the laugh of a child playing innocently and there is heaven in it. We see a painting of misty mountains on an unknown horizon and we can picture it beyond the mountains. Some say it is there, to the West, beyond the journeys of men, and we can almost believe it. As Melville said, "There is something magic in it."

CHAPTER 2

The Vision of Prophets

Moses, lawgiver and prophet, the first prophet.[1] A prophet in the cultures around Israel was usually a paid lackey for the king. Moses' example took prophecy to a new level for Israel. Moses was no false prophet to an imaginary god. He didn't read calf livers or keep books of omens for use in soothsaying. He was a visionary, a mouthpiece for God.

And so the prophets in Israel were successors of Moses. God took a common Near Eastern institution and made something true and good out of it.

The prophets of Israel had a message of justice. They called Israel to faithfulness to God's Torah. They railed against cruelty, selfishness, abuse, and injustice. They delivered messages of hope for the faithful. Delayed hope. But hope that people of faith could cling to.

They were singers of songs that came true, writers of poetry that would surely find fulfillment. Those poems often contained messages of hope that were not realized in the lifetime of the prophet or his audience.

Delayed hope. It challenges our faith. Is it hope that never comes? Should we believe in something an unknown person said 3,000 years ago? We could use some hope, but the world seems a cruel place. In fact, God himself seems heartless.

Surprisingly, the prophets of Israel were quite realistic about this. They didn't try to hide the pain of life in the real world. The hope they offered was not mindless optimism. The voice of biblical hope even dares to ask God, "How long?"

Isaiah spoke of Israel being sore head to foot, bruised and hurting. He said, "Your land is desolate, your cities are burned to the ground; foreigners devour your land in your presence; it's as desolate as if overwhelmed by floods."[2]

It's easy to read a verse like this and underestimate the pain felt by those who experienced it. When Isaiah spoke of burned cities, his audience carried painful memories of dead loved ones, even dead children. Some were children without parents. People who had once been happy lost land and life to foreign invaders.

Prophets, from Moses to Isaiah to Malachi, were realistic about the pains of this life. Yet they also promised a future hope. For the faithful, who could believe in the midst of suffering, this future hope would make present pain more bearable. Moses, the prototypical prophet, first set the pattern with a vision of coming pain and future hope.

Moses' greatest vision came near the end of the forty-year wilderness experience. The first generation was nearly all dead. A new generation prepared to enter the Promised Land. Moses saw doom and restoration, failure from the beginning but redemption at the end.

HOPE AFTER HOPELESSNESS

How would you like to be told from the beginning of a covenant with God that you would fail? In a prophecy later echoed in the words of other prophets, Deuteronomy 30:1-6 sets the pattern for history.

Moses had just explained what blessings Israel could experience and what curses would come from unfaithfulness. The nation would have rain, blessing, and life if the people followed God's Torah. They would have the most awful curses, so awful they are painful to read, if they did not.

The curses of Deuteronomy do not represent God's cruelty. They represent man's. Yet if the people disobeyed the Torah, God would hand them over to their own cruelty and the cruelty of conquering nations. Starvation. Children dying. War. Mothers eating the bodies of their dead children to survive. Unbearable pain.

And God gave Moses the message: all these things will come upon you.

From the beginning, standing on the threshold of the Promised Land, the children of those who had left Egypt discovered that they would fail. Moses said, "When all these things come upon you, the blessing and the curse . . ."[3] There would be no avoiding the curse, the curse for disobeying God's covenant. Doom was inevitable.

Yet Moses' vision was not really about the doom, but the hope at the end. Life is often unbearable pain. People of faith need to know that there is hope for the future. This is God's promise through Moses and the prophets.

A day was coming when Israel would be dramatically changed. The people would be purified. God would circumcise them, not their foreskins but their hearts. At last, Israel would love God heart, mind, and soul.[4]

The vision that Moses had was foundational. Other prophets would expand on it.[5] Israel's history would be a little blessing, a lot of curse, scattering to the farthest places under heaven, remembering God, returning to the land, and one day . . . blessing beyond all imagination. Failure. Exile. Restoration. Blessing beyond imagination.

Well, the prophets did a lot of imagining. What would that blessing be like?

THE WORLD IN EXILE

Israel's experience mirrors the world's experience. We live in a world in exile. We are surrounded by the sad and disturbing. We are experiencing the curse. We need the hope of future blessing. The curse is why many do not believe God is real.

Evolution is a view that fits our reality in many ways. Animals mate brutally and without romance. Evolution tells we are merely animals. So we mate brutally. Only we are killing some part of us in so doing.

Animals die largely unmourned. So in our animal reality death reigns. Competition is the game of life. Survival of the fittest is our experience. The stronger rise and the weaker fall. Yet even that principle can be broken, for "under the sun the race is not to the swift, nor the battle to the strong."[6] No wonder so many of our neighbors cannot see God or grace in Creation.

Looking out from this exile in the land of godlessness, we need a vision of days to come. It might be hard to believe the vision from our place of exile. We see a beautiful wood but we know inside there are briers and poison plants and snakes. We enjoy a clear river, but we know about pollution and wouldn't dare drink from it. We admire an animal, but we know it might either kill one of us or one of us might kill it.

We want to believe in life but we see too much death. Can God and cancer be true at the same time? Sometimes we can ignore the hurting around us and we say, "Let's eat and drink now, because tomorrow we'll be dead!"[7] Other times, we feel the pain and we can identify with Job who said, "My days pass more swiftly than a weaver's shuttle and come to their end without hope."[8] The view from here can be hopeless.

That is because we do not see far. Lost in the woods, we might try climbing a tall tree to look in all directions for some way out. Where is there a tower to climb and survey the past and future? For those willing to believe, the prophets are such a tower, giving us a vantage point high above this world in exile.

Israel needed Moses' vision of future hope in Deuteronomy 30:1-6. So we need the vision of Moses and the prophets, a vision of a better World to Come.

AMOS AND THE PLOWMAN

Amos was a sheepherder from Tekoa,[9] a town in Judah in the south. God didn't send Amos to his own people in Judah, but sent him north to the kingdom of Israel. Amos spoke to the northern tribes of Israel about one generation before Assyria came and destroyed them all.

Not only did Amos have a lot to say about justice rolling like an ever-flowing stream, but God also gave him a vision of the future. Amos spoke about "that day," a favorite expression of the prophets.[10] That day is the coming age when God will act and bring Israel and the world out of exile. Amos saw it because God showed him a little piece of it.

In the little piece that God showed Amos, several things will happen. The *sukkah* (or booth) of David will be repaired, the nations will be called by God's name, the plowman will overtake the reaper, the mountains will drip sweet wine, and Israel will be forever restored from captivity.

A *sukkah* is a booth made of branches, usually used as a shelter in the fields for the workers to get some shade from the sun. It is also used at the Feast of Booths, also called Tabernacles or *Sukkot*. God will restore the doomed throne of David, the line of Messiah in that day. When that happens, Israel will possess the nations.

Israel possessing the nations might sound like bad news for non-Jews but the news is really good. Amos explains that, in that day, Gentiles will be called by God's name. That is, God does not plan to limit his restorative joy to Israel, but will call Gentiles into relationship as well.[11]

I can totally get into the paradise Amos painted for us of the World to Come, the picture of mountains dripping wine and plowmen overtaking reapers. I have experienced a foretaste of this world already.

I travel to Israel at least once a year. I have seen the terraced hillsides in Judah, where vineyards and orchards seem unlikely. The terrain is very steep and rocky, with unending hills and small mountains. But grapes grow on them. There are vines scattered here and there on the rocky mountains. Yet in that day, the grapes will be so abundant, the mountains will literally drip with sweet wine. Paradise.

The rabbis take the vision a step further. They paint a fanciful but desirable picture of this grape paradise:

Not like this world will be the World to Come. In this world one has the trouble to harvest grapes and to press them; but in the World to Come a person will bring a single grape in a wagon or a ship, store it in the corner of his house, and draw from it enough wine to fill a large flagon ... There will not be a grape which will not yield thirty measures of wine.[12]

What about the plowman overtaking the reaper? What does that mean? There will be so much fruit and grain that before it can all be harvested, it will be time to plant a new crop. Again the rabbis fill out this image of plenty:"As in this world grain is produced after six months and trees grow fruit after twelve months, in the hereafter grain will be produced after one month and trees will grow fruit after two months."[13]

All nations will know God and plowmen will overtake reapers. To modify John Lennon's famous line, imagine there's no hunger and no secularism too. That is the vision of Amos. That day will not be a world in the clouds or some existence on another plane. That day will be heaven on earth.

TEMPLE AND TORAH

The last time the world saw God's holy Temple was in 70 C.E. That was the year the Romans came and tore it stone from stone, just as Yeshua had foretold.[14] I have been many times to Jerusalem to the South Wall excavations where tourists can see an excavated pile of stones from the time of Herod. Until the last part of the twentieth century this massive pile of stones was underground, covered by the centuries of growth in Jerusalem. Now the pile of stones once smoothed by skilled masons and later roughly cast down by Roman soldiers is visible.

In December of 2004, I was leading a tour group on the Temple Mount in Jerusalem. I like to think that God gave us a moment of happy coincidence. Something significant was going on that day, right at the very time we were on the Temple Mount. There were ten times as many police out as usual. We looked for signs and protesters but we saw none. What was going on?

Our tour guide could not get the police to tell him. They just said it was perfectly safe for our group to go on the Temple Mount, so we went. Once we were up there, our tour guide was stunned. We saw ultra-Orthodox Jewish men walking on the platform where the Temple once stood. He explained that usually this is forbidden by Jewish law lest a person tread on the place where the Holy of Holies used to be.

So what were these religious men doing here? No one would tell us anything. We found out when we got home and read the Jerusalem Post. These men were the newly formed Sanhedrin, the council of seventy, and they were taking some measurements on the Temple Mount. The measurements had to do with their theories about where the Temple should be rebuilt.

In the prophets' vision of the age to come the Temple is always there. Isaiah says:

> It shall come to pass in the latter days
> that the mountain of the house of [Adonai]
> shall be established as the highest of the mountains,
> and shall be lifted up above the hills;
> and all the nations shall flow to it,
> and many peoples shall come, and say:
> "Come, let us go up to the mountain of [Adonai],
> to the house of the God of Jacob,
> that he may teach us his ways
> and that we may walk in his paths."
> For out of Zion shall go the law,
> and the word of [Adonai] from Jerusalem.[15]

The house of Adonai is the Temple. The word of Adonai is the Torah. Isaiah says the age to come will be an age with Torah and Temple.[16]

Again, we might suspect that the prophets envisioned a world just like the one they knew. Perhaps they could not comprehend a world without Torah and Temple. Perhaps they were unaware that in Christendom these symbols would have little or no value. Perhaps they were unaware that many of God's followers would one day view Torah and Temple as relics of an outdated religion. Yet, on the other hand, maybe we should be students of the prophets and not the other way around. Maybe we simply have trouble envisioning a world different than our own.

What is old and what is new? Will some of the old be reclaimed in the new? I think so. Take the New Covenant. It has the word new in it. Yet, when you learn about it, you find it also has some old things in it. It is something few understand.

Is the Torah part of the New Covenant or is it old and past its time? Jeremiah saw Torah in the New Covenant. In the very passage where Jeremiah gave the world the concept of a New Covenant, he reported God's words: "I will put my Torah within them and write it on their hearts; I will be their God, and they will be my people."[17] Ezekiel saw the same thing. In that day, God said through Ezekiel, "I will put my Spirit inside you and cause you to live by my laws, respect my rulings and obey them."[18]

The Torah is one of the old things that will be fully realized in the new.

What about that Temple in the age to come? Do we learn more about it? Actually, Ezekiel described it in detail, even giving measurements.[19] In the same chapters where Ezekiel describes a lot of detail about the land of Israel in the days of Messiah, he tells us how wide the walls, doorways, and rooms of the Temple and the Temple Mount will be at that time. An architect can produce a relatively complete model from Ezekiel's description.

The Temple, like the Torah, is one of the old things that will be even more glorious in the new.[20]

TIKKUN OLAM IN THE PROPHETS

Tikkun Olam (ti-KOON oh-LOMM) means repairing the world.[21] It is a popular catch phrase among Jews with a vision to leave the world better than they found it. The World to Come is a world repaired from a thousand oppressions and injustices, which the prophets of Israel railed against. Tikkun Olam involves bringing justice to the oppressed, comfort to mourners, and returning good in place of evil.

The prophets envisioned a World to Come where the oppressed find justice and righteousness. When Messiah comes, Isaiah 11:3-4 tells us, he will judge fairly and will right the wrongs experienced by the poor and the meek. Similarly, Isaiah 61 tells us that Messiah encourages the afflicted, comfort for mourners, and freedom for those in bondage.

It is a common mistake to assume that since God will do all these things in the World to Come that they are his responsibility and not ours. That is, we might sit on our hands waiting for God to bring justice and goodness in the world. This is a reaction we might expect from people who know that God alone can fix what is broken in our world. Since we can't fix it all, shouldn't we just wait on God? What good are our contributions anyway?

This is not at all what the prophets (much less Yeshua)[22] came to teach. The prophets charged Israel with failure to establish righteousness and justice in the land. The Hebrew word for righteousness is *tzedekah*. Norman Snaith demonstrates that the word's original meaning is "to be straight."[23] Things in the land had become crooked, with needy people being used by the wealthy for personal gain. God called all the nation of Israel to respond: the crooked must be straightened. The land must be repaired.

Amos denounced his generation because they "sell the upright for silver and the poor for a pair of shoes, grinding the heads of the poor in the dust."[24] Yet they continued worshipping God at the Temple as though their callous disregard for the poor would not affect their relationship with God. Amos's instruction was severe: "Spare me the noise of your songs!. . . . Instead, let justice well up like water, and righteousness like an ever-flowing stream."[25]

Similarly, Isaiah called for Judah to develop a new kind of fast. Instead of appearing to be religious and humble, Isaiah told his generation:

> Here is the sort of fast I want—releasing those unjustly bound, untying the thongs of the yoke, letting the oppressed go free, breaking every yoke, sharing your food with the hungry, taking the homeless poor into your house, clothing the naked when you see them, fulfilling your duty to your kinsmen.[26]

Hosea called for a religion that was more about *hesed*, covenant love for God and fellow man, than sacrifice.[27] Micah said that loving justice and *hesed* was the kind of religion God required of his generation.[28] It is clear that the prophets promised a future free from oppression and hunger. Yet they did not call on God's people to merely await that day. They called for Israel to work to make it happen in their own time.

The truth about Tikkun Olam is that we will not achieve it. We cannot feed everyone. But we can feed someone. We cannot stop all injustice. But we can speak up for justice. It should be those who believe most in the World to Come who seek to bring as much of it as possible into this present world.

THE PROPHETIC WORLD TO COME

One of my favorite expressions about the World to Come is from Micah, a prophet who was a contemporary to Isaiah. He said: "They shall sit every man under his vine and under his fig tree, and no one shall make them afraid."[29] God's idea of the World to Come is people with their own vine and fig tree. It was a common expression in biblical times for peace and prosperity. The prophets envisioned an agricultural paradise in the World to Come. Who are we to gainsay the word of God? Maybe the agricultural part is literal. Even if it is not, I am in love with God's plan that the World to Come has mountains, rivers, and trees.

This is not the view of witless shadows in a murky world or disembodied spirits on the Blessed Isles. This is not the view of white-robed saints playing harps on clouds (who made that up anyway?). In the prophetic vision, the good things of this world are better in the World to Come.

That is a meaningful statement. The good things of this world are better in the World to Come. C. S. Lewis captured the image beautifully in his book The Great Divorce. Busloads of residents from hell get a field trip to heaven (just go with the fiction here and don't worry about whether the story is literal). As the tourists get off the bus, they appear transparent. They cannot move the slenderest blade of grass. In fact, they are like ghosts and the grass appears through their feet as if they were made of mist. Then the protagonist realizes something; the people are not ghosts. They are the same as they have always been. It is heaven that is different:

The men were as they had always been; as all the men I had known had been perhaps. It was the light, the grass, the trees that were different; made of some different substance, so much solider than things in our country that men were ghosts by comparison.[30]

The World to Come is like our world only better. Perhaps, as Lewis imagined, even the light will be better.

We really should not be surprised by this physicality. It is what God expressed in the beginning. In Genesis 1 he said over and over, "It is good." Before Adam and Eve fell they had "every tree that is pleasant to the sight and good for food."[31] Only afterwards would agriculture be a backbreaking chore and childbirth a pain almost to death.

That means we were not so wrong when a landscape painting awoke in us a desire for heaven. The romantic feelings we felt about some faerie land or about Narnia or Middle Earth or a Disney scene were a longing to be where we are intended to be. We are not wrong when we admire the ocean or a tall hill and dream of adventure. We were made for paradise after all.

CHAPTER 3

Israel as the Vessel

T he story of God and Abraham is unusual to say the least. If God ever befriended a man, it was Abraham. There was nothing obvious about Abraham that made him such a unique choice. Yet what other man, except Yeshua, has been so highly favored by God? God's promises to Abraham, often repeated in Genesis, are unique: a blessed line, a blessing to all nations, and a blessed name.

As Orthodox Jewish theologian Michael Wyschogrod asserts, God's plan to bless the world through Abraham is a foolproof plan.[1] The plan does not depend on any human response or responsibility. God's plan depends only on birth—that a line of descendants would be born starting with Abraham. Since being born is one thing we cannot interfere with, God's plan depends only on his own power and wisdom.

REDEMPTION AND CONSUMMATION THROUGH A PEOPLE

What exactly is God's plan? There is no one place in the Bible to find it. Some of us would like for the Bible to have a book called "First Theologian" or "The Chronicle of Answers." No such book exists. God's plan comes through a story. God's story for us starts with Creation, though hints of time before that show through in some places. In places we get a glance at time before time. Neither does God's story end with Yeshua's resurrection and ascension. In places we get a glance at the glorious future.

The great thing about a story is that it has far more depth than a set of propositions or facts. Stories have layers of meaning and varying perspectives. You could imagine the story of Creation from God's point of view, Adam's, Eve's, the serpent's, or the angels'. A good story hints at more than the mere words can tell.

The problem with a story is that interpretation can be difficult. It is too easy to read a story with a particular preconceived idea and to find that very idea in the story. It is easy to read a story from the wrong point of view.

Let me suggest that the story of the Bible is often read from the wrong point of view. A religious Jew might read the story as if the characters are Orthodox Jews. A Christian tends to read the story as if the characters are Christians.

R. Kendall Soulen is a theologian with a powerful message. He is calling for the Church to read the Bible as if it is God's plan to work through Israel for the world. Soulen coined a helpful term: the canonical narrative.[2] The canon is another word for the writings contained in the Bible. To read the Bible as one story, the whole canon unified in accepting this one story, is to have a canonical narrative.

The problem is that the typical canonical narrative of the Church has left Israel out. In fact, the primary point of the Bible as held by influential church fathers and many theologians and writers since would be just fine if the Old Testament ended at Genesis 4:1. Very little in much of Christian theology would be affected if the Bible were cut down to the New Testament plus Genesis 1–3 as a prologue.

The typical Christian way of viewing the Bible's main story, the canonical narrative, is as follows: God made everything good, Adam and Eve brought on the Fall of Creation, Jesus came to redeem sin, and Jesus will return to consummate the world (to finalize and perfect the paradise God had planned from the beginning). To put it briefly, the standard canonical narrative is: Creation (Gen. 1-2), Fall (Gen. 3), Redemption, and Consummation.[3] In this scheme, Israel is a mere footnote.

Bible readers coming from a Christian point of view have always struggled with the question: "What do we do with Israel?" Even the least educated reader of the Bible learns pretty quickly that it is a Jewish book.

The beauty of God's story is that it is far wiser and more subtly brilliant than we can conceive. I suggest we follow a different principle than the standard canonical narrative. I suggest we see Israel as the center of God's plan and not the periphery. I suggest that we try to understand Israel not as a footnote, but as the protagonist, the chief player, the lead actor.

ISRAEL AND THE BIBLE'S STORY

To properly understand that Bible's story, the canonical narrative, it is vital to realize something from the beginning. Creation was good, but not yet perfect.[4]

Sometimes people think God is restoring the world to the way it was before the Fall, before the disobedience of Adam and Eve. Actually, God had something better in mind from the beginning. Adam and Eve needed two things for sure: immortality and knowledge. So God planted two trees to provide them. He allowed them only to partake of immortality, but theologians have long suspected he had a plan to bring them knowledge in the course of time. God walked with Adam. He had some things to teach. There was more, but people were not yet ready.

Before this could happen, and none of this caught God by surprise, Adam and Eve brought the world further from consummation, not closer. The action of the first man and woman brought fundamental changes in Creation, changes rightly called the Fall.

After the Fall, the waywardness of humankind is obvious. Murder, lust, greed, and a desire for power and domination rule the earth. Even a flood only slows it down. Even scattering people and confusing their languages is only a stopgap measure. God must have another plan.

Is God's choice the one you or I would have made? Would we have had the wisdom to know that the best way to move into redemption and to consummate the world was to choose one man and create a human-proof plan?

God chose Abraham, a herdsman of some wealth and a pagan. If nothing else, the placement of the Abraham story should tell us that this is not an incidental, but a crucial step in God's plan. God's plan was to choose Israel as his vessel.

This may sound narrow, but here on earth, Israel is the vessel of God through which he is bringing redemption and consummation. Obviously, through Israel God already brought the scriptures and the Messiah. But God is not done. He is still using Israel as his vessel. Redemption is available through Israel's Son, Yeshua, but redemption is not complete. God has more people and more of Creation yet to save. Further, God is not merely redeeming, but he is bringing all things to a world better than at Creation. The World to Come is greater than this world, and even greater than the world before the Fall.

How is God doing all this through Israel? Israel is his vessel. Israel is the priestly people, a calling that is shared by Yeshua-followers but is still not taken away from Israel. And Israel is at the center of all God's covenants, his great and wise actions that bring redemption and consummation of all things.

God's first formal covenant was with Noah, encompassing all of humankind. Yet there is nothing salvific in the covenant with Noah. It is with Abraham that redemption and consummation began to be worked out.

Through Abraham, God established a way of looking at humankind that remains to this day: Israel and the nations. In the covenant with Abraham, there are the descendants of Abraham, the blessed line, and all other peoples, blessed through Abraham's line. God's blessing comes through Abraham, through Israel, and through no other avenue.

God further advanced his covenant plan to redeem through the Sinai Covenant. The covenant given through Moses was about Israel being a priestly people, a people who showed God to the nations. You see this aspect of God's plan not only in Exodus 19, but also throughout the Psalms and prophets (do a concordance search on "the nations").

Some people think the Sinai Covenant is over and done with. Israel failed and that covenant is nothing but a fossil. Yet if you read the Sinai Covenant, you find that failure was built into the plan from the beginning.[5]

What few Christian readers know is that the next major covenant, the New Covenant, was also made with Israel. Just to be clear, Jeremiah says, "I will make a new covenant with the house of Israel and the house of Judah."[6] This is why the New Testament goes to great lengths dealing with Gentiles being "grafted in" and included in the promises through Yeshua.

Just in case anyone is unclear, and some in the early Roman church were unclear about this, Paul clarifies: God is still in covenant with Israel, yes, even non-believing Israel. Paul says, "God has not rejected his people whom he foreknew" and though "they are enemies of God for your sake" nonetheless "as regards election, they are beloved for the sake of the fathers."[7]

Israel is God's vessel, the lead actor in the canonical narrative. The canonical narrative is not finished. God has more to do. He has hinted at the future and we know what he has allowed us to glance at, but more of the story remains to be written. We should not be surprised that Israel is still the center of the story (don't worry, the next chapter will be about the nations).

ISRAEL AND THE AGE TO COME

Virtually all of the promises of the age to come occur in Israel, with Israel as the central player. Again, we might assume that this was due to the audience's limitation in understanding. Jewish prophets spoke about future Israel because Israel was being addressed. On the other hand, as I have said before, it may be that we need to orient ourselves to the Bible's perspective rather than translating it to our own.

When Yeshua returns, it will be to Israel. When Yeshua returns, the specific event that draws him will be Israel's need for rescue in a gruesome war commonly known as Armageddon. "Then ADONAI will go out and fight against those nations, fighting as on a day of battle," and "his feet will stand on the Mount of Olives."[8]

Consider the basic plot of the end of this age and the beginning of the age to come. You can see more detail and a more complete list of prophecies in "Appendix A: Scripture Compendium." For the moment, I simply want to introduce the drama and quote biblical language about the World to Come.

Israel will be drawn back into the land: "He will return and gather you from all the peoples to which ADONAI your God scattered you. If one of yours was scattered to the far end of the sky, ADONAI your God will gather you even from there; he will go there and get you."[9]

Armies from the nations will attack Israel: "I will gather all the nations against Jerusalem to battle."[10]

God will trap these armies, luring them to attack Israel: "I will gather all the nations and bring them down to the Valley of Jehoshaphat [Adonai judges]."[11]

God will destroy those armies and rescue Israel: "Swing the sickle, for the harvest is ripe; come, and tread, for the winepress is full. The vats are overflowing, for their wickedness is great."[12]

Yeshua himself will be Israel's deliverer: "For I tell you, from now on, you will not see me again until you say, 'Blessed is he who comes in the name of ADONAI.'"[13]

God will restore the tribal lands in Israel: "These are the borders of the land you are to distribute for inheritance by the twelve tribes of Israel."[14]

Jerusalem will become the center of the world: "It shall come to pass in the latter days that the mountain of the house of [Adonai] shall be established as the highest of the mountains, and shall be lifted up above the hills; and all the nations shall flow to it."[15]

The Torah will be given to the nations: "Many peoples shall come, and say: 'Come, let us go up to the mountain of [Adonai], to the house of the God of Jacob, that he may teach us his ways and that we may walk in his paths.' For out of Zion shall go the law, and the word of [Adonai] from Jerusalem."[16]

Non-Jews will attach themselves to Jews in order to find God: "When that time comes, ten men will take hold—speaking all the languages of the nations—will grab hold of the cloak of a Jew and say, 'We want to go with you, because we have heard that God is with you.'"[17]

Nations will be included with Israel as God's people: "In that day Israel will be the third with Egypt and Assyria, a blessing in the midst of the earth, whom [Adonai] of hosts has blessed, saying, 'Blessed be Egypt my people, and Assyria the work of my hands, and Israel my inheritance.'"[18]

The hearts of Israel will be made new, circumcised, and filled with Torah: "I will give you a new heart and put a new spirit inside you; I will take the stony heart out of your flesh and give you a heart of flesh. I will put my Spirit inside you and cause you to live by my laws, respect my rulings and obey them."[19]

A river of life will flow from the Temple in Jerusalem to the Dead Sea, which will become alive: "On both riverbanks will grow all kinds of trees for food; their leaves will not dry up, nor will their fruit fail. There will be a different kind of fruit each month, because the water flows from the sanctuary, so that this fruit will be edible, and the leaves will have healing properties."[20]

Messiah Yeshua will rule from David's throne in Jerusalem: "Of the increase of his government and of peace there will be no end, on the throne of David and over his kingdom, to establish it and to uphold it with justice and with righteousness from this time forth and forevermore."[21]

There will be sacrifices and priests serving in God's Temple: "The Levitical priests shall never lack a man in my presence to offer burnt offerings, to burn grain offerings, and to make sacrifices forever."[22]

God will dwell with Israel forever: "Son of man, this is the place of my throne and the place of the soles of my feet, where I will dwell in the midst of the people of Israel forever."[23]

GOD'S VESSEL CANNOT FAIL

God loved Abraham. Through him, God created a vessel for redemption and consummation. God redeems the world through the drama of Israel and will perfect the world in the same way. None of God's plan depends on individuals obeying and making his plan happen. God's plan is foolproof.

"For I know what plans I have in mind for you," God says to Israel, "plans for well-being, not for bad things; so that you can have hope and a future."[24] Ultimately these verses are more than a word to Jeremiah's generation about hope after despair. Ultimately they describe the center of the canonical narrative. Through Israel, Yeshua came. He brings wholeness. He is a future and hope for Israel and the nations.

And to the nations we will turn next. God did not plan to use his vessel Israel only to redeem and perfect Israel. God has a plan for Israel and the nations.

CHAPTER 4

The Nations as the Goal

The wheat farmer in China and the mountain villager in Khazakstan, the goat herder in Jordan and the bushman in Botswana, the commodities trader in Chicago and the cab driver in London—God sees each one and loves. "What is man that you are mindful of him?" the Psalmist asks God. "Yet you have made him a little lower than the heavenly beings and crowned him with glory and honor," he continues.[1] The text actually says "a little lower than God," but translators often choose the less controversial possibility "heavenly beings."

There is something different in the Creation account about the stars and the humans, the mountains and the babies, the ocean and a woman. The stars were spoken into being, as were the ocean and the mountains. But a man or woman or child began with a divine sculpture, formed from the clay.[2] Mount Everest may be inspiring, but it is not made in God's image and likeness, neither is the Grand Canyon.

In his book, *Sex God*, Rob Bell describes a safari trip he made with his family.[3] They witnessed a pride of lions and saw a male mating with a female. It was a rough affair, lacking tenderness—a business transaction in an animalistic way. The lioness did not say to the lion, "Wait, before we do this, do you love me? Will you care for me and our cubs?" The lion did not paw her hair tenderly and say, "You are the one I was made for." Even a majestic animal like a lion lacks the spiritual nature and intellectual depth that makes man a marvel. Lions are made far below God, not merely a little.

The grandeur of all humankind is a teaching of the Bible. God's love has never been limited to one group within humanity. Rather, through one group, Israel, God's love enters the world in a tangible way: through prophets and apostles and ultimately through Messiah.

Many of God's great declarations of love in the Bible are directed specifically to Israel and not to all humankind. He says to

Israel, "I love you with an everlasting love."[4] He speaks tenderly to his wayward wife Israel and says:

> How can I give you up, O Ephraim?
> How can I hand you over, O Israel?
> How can I make you like Admah?
> How can I treat you like Zeboiim?
> My heart recoils within me;
> my compassion grows warm and tender.[5]

Passages like these gave rise to a problem of interpretation. When Jews brought the Bible to non-Jews, confusion started very early. When a non-Jew reads his or her Bible, it is with certainty that the everlasting love of God is for him or her too. So how do we interpret and teach these passages?

The common approach is to ignore the original intent. The love letter to Israel is appropriated by non-Israel. A pastor preaches Jeremiah 31:3 as God's love for all. A youth pastor puts a poster of Jeremiah 29:11 on the wall. It's a bit like stealing a line from someone else's love letter and addressing it to yourself or to someone else.

But what are non-Jews to do? The Bible should not be a book just for Jews, should it? God made us all just a little lower than himself, right?

Indeed, and there is a way to be true to the Bible and see God's everlasting love for all nations, tribes, and tongues. Yes, God loves Israel in an intimate way, but he has always planned to bring the nations in. It has always been there, and like two different children of the same father, we are both loved, Israel and the nations.

ABRAHAM, JOSEPH, AND MOSES

A man had two sons, one older and one younger. He said to the first, "I am going to help you prosper and succeed in my business, but I am not doing this only for you. I am going to bless your younger brother through you. You must not forget why you are prospering."

So God said to Abraham, "I will make your name great."[6] He also said, "In you all the families of the earth will be blessed."[7] The principle is that the one who blesses Abraham's children will be blessed and the one who curses will be cursed.[8] This is a principle of relationship, the younger brother's prospering tied to the older brother, with the same father.

God demonstrates the principle several times in the stories of Abraham and his sons. A foreign king unknowingly takes Sarah to be in his harem and God threatens him.[9] Isaac grows mightier than the local king because God is blessing him. The king sends Isaac away fearing a war, but later the king makes a covenant with Isaac. He says, "We saw very clearly that Adonai has been with you."[10]

The story of Abraham's children and the nations is especially demonstrated in the life of Joseph. Joseph is sold into the nations, but rises to prominence because of God's covenant blessing. Soon the nations face a famine, but they come to Joseph, the seed of Abraham, to be rescued.[11] Blessing comes to the nations through Israel. This is God's pattern.

In any given generation, the pattern does not necessarily work. The older brother, Israel, forgets why he is prospering. The younger brother grows mighty and persecutes the older brother. All sorts of things go wrong. But the pattern will come out in the end. It is God's foolproof plan. The younger brother will be blessed through the older.

At the end of the Torah, Moses sang a prophetic song. It is a somewhat difficult poem and many modern readers have little patience with poetry. Yet, if you take the time, Deuteronomy 32 is comprehensible. And in it, God said through Moses, "I will make them jealous with those who are no people; I will provoke them to anger with a foolish nation."[12]

It is the same principle Paul declares in Romans 11:11. In the time of the older brother's folly, God will use the younger brother to win him back. The nations need Israel, and Israel needs the nations. From the beginning, God has had a place for the nations in mind. From the Chinese wheat farmer to the Botswanian bushman, God loves with everlasting love.

THE NATIONS IN TORAH AND PROPHECY

There are a number of myths and understandings about Gentiles and the Torah. Many people think Gentiles were called unclean in the writings of Moses and kept away from God. Part of this confusion comes from the Judaism in the time of the New Testament. The Temple then had a court of the Gentiles, which kept Gentiles far away. Strict Jewish practice in the New Testament era regarded Gentiles as unclean. But God never said this.

In Torah, there were three ways Gentiles were included: assimilation, participation, and invitation. By assimilation, I mean that a large number of Gentiles became part of Israel, such as Caleb the Kenizzite (not an Israelite by birth) and the mixed multitude at the Exodus. By participation, I mean the sojourner who lived with the Israelites and yet remained separate. He was invited to offer sacrifices and participate almost fully.[13] Though not in the Torah proper, Solomon's prayer in 1 Kings 8 shows the principle of invitation.[14] Solomon prayed that the prayers of foreigners, directed toward God's Temple in Jerusalem, would be heard in heaven. Gentiles could join Israel, worship with Israel, or at the very least, pray to Israel's God.

It is in the Psalms and the Prophets that we begin to see a major theme of God's love spreading from Israel to the nations to the ends of the earth:

David recognized God's plan for Israel's worship to spread to the nations: "All the ends of the earth will remember and turn to ADONAI; all the clans of the nations will worship in your presence. For the kingdom belongs to ADONAI, and he rules the nations."[15]

Israel recognized that the nations would be drawn to God through them: "Let the nations be glad and shout for joy, for you will judge the peoples fairly and guide the nations on earth. Let the peoples give thanks to you, God; let the peoples give thanks to you, all of them. The earth has yielded its harvest; may God, our God, bless us. May God continue to bless us, so that all the ends of the earth will fear him."[16]

Various prayers for all the nations to know God: "May his name endure forever, his fame continue as long as the sun! May people be blessed in him, all nations call him blessed!"[17]

Non-Jews are received as Non-Jews, and not expected to convert: "In that day I will raise up the booth of David that is fallen and repair its breaches, and raise up its ruins and rebuild it as in the days of old, that they may possess the remnant of Edom and all the nations who are called by my name."[18]

The nations will come up to Jerusalem to learn the Torah and to worship God: "It shall come to pass in the latter days that the mountain of the house of [Adonai] shall be established as the highest of the mountains, and shall be lifted up above the hills; and all the nations shall flow to it, and many peoples shall come, and say: 'Come, let us go up to the mountain of [Adonai], to the house of the God of Jacob, that he may teach us his ways and that we may walk in his paths.'"[19]

Messiah comes for the nations: "I will give you as a covenant for the people, a light for the nations, to open the eyes that are blind, to bring out the prisoners from the dungeon, from the prison those who sit in darkness."[20] "It is too light a thing that you should be my servant to raise up the tribes of Jacob and to bring back the preserved of Israel; I will make you as a light for the nations, that my salvation may reach to the end of the earth."[21]

Israel's restoration will draw nations to God: "Nations will go toward your light and kings toward your shining splendor."[22]

Some from the nations will serve as Levites and Priests in God's Temple: "They shall declare my glory among the nations. And they shall bring all your brothers from all the nations as an offering to [Adonai], on horses and in chariots and in litters and on mules and on dromedaries, to my holy mountain Jerusalem, says [Adonai], just as the Israelites bring their grain offering in a clean vessel to the house of [Adonai]. And some of them also I will take for priests and for Levites, says [Adonai]."[23]

The nations who attack Israel will be cursed: "I will gather all the nations and bring them down to the Valley of Jehoshaphat. And I will enter into judgment with them there, on behalf of my people and my heritage Israel, because they have scattered them among the nations and have divided up my land, and have cast lots for my people, and have traded a boy for a prostitute, and have sold a girl for wine and have drunk it."[24]

Many from the nations will attach themselves to Israel to find God: "When that time comes, ten men will take hold—speaking all the languages of the nations - will grab hold of the cloak of a Jew and say, "We want to go with you, because we have heard that God is with you.'"[25]

The nations will worship God at the Temple with Israel at the Feasts: "Then everyone who survives of all the nations that have come against Jerusalem shall go up year after year to worship the King, [Adonai] of hosts, and to keep the Feast of Booths."[26]

THE FINAL CHAPTERS OF THE STORY: ISRAEL AND THE NATIONS

What God loves he cares for. His own image and likeness is found in every family in the earth. Love for the older brother does not remove love for the younger. Rather, by prospering the older brother, God is bringing the younger brother blessing as well.

So far, the story since Yeshua's day has been more one of the younger brother receiving the blessing. Countless millions of Gentiles have been touched by God's forgiving love. The older brother brought the scriptures and the Messiah to the younger. And all over the world, the blessing of the younger brother can be seen. Chinese wheat farmers know the God of Israel and so do Botswanian bushmen. The older brother, right now, is in need of the help of the younger. Israel is largely in unbelief, while a good portion of the nations believe.

Yet the story of Israel and the nations is more complex than the simple analogy of the two brothers. Right now there are some in Israel who have received the full blessing, believing in Messiah and inheriting the World to Come. At the same time, there are some of the nations who have rejected Israel, refusing to acknowledge that the blessing came from them and will continue to come from them.

The drama of Israel and the nations has an interesting future with tragedy and joy. The various stages of that drama that are being played out and will be played out are:

1. The regathering of Israel into the land.
2. Strife between Israel and the nations.
3. Armageddon, the great battle when the nations send armies to attack Israel.

4. The return of God to this earth to rescue his people Israel.
5. The drawing of the nations to God through Israel.
6. The reign of Israel's Messiah for a thousand years.
7. The Temple and Torah spreading to all the peoples in Messiah's reign.
8. The final battle at the end of the thousand years.
9. The Final Age, the New Jerusalem, also called the New Heavens and the New Earth, without Temple but with all righteousness forever.

God will recover and redeem all that he loves, both Israel and the nations. The older and younger brother will be reconciled. In that day, "[t]hen Adonai will be king over the whole world. On that day Adonai will be the only one, and his name will be the only name."[27]

CHAPTER 5

Yeshua and the Kingdom of God

Talk about him was everywhere. A charismatic healer from the north, they had heard of his sort before. He was great at telling stories and amusing the rabble of the land. These holy men were usually short on education but long on popularity. This one had thousands sitting on hillsides as he wove stories and captivated their peasant minds. The council had sent emissaries to determine if he was a threat.

He claimed that the time they were all waiting for was about to arrive. It was right at hand. His message was not revolution, but repentance. Around this simple message he gathered disciples who looked just like the simple masses following him.

What did this would-be messiah think would happen? How would he and his band be part of bringing the coming age of Israel's restoration? What was his plan? Were they secretly arming themselves? Were they allied with zealots and brigands? Some said one of his disciples was a zealot. Worse yet, an eyewitness told the council this one spoke about the Temple being destroyed. What crazy idea was this?

Even now the holy man was speaking to a crowd. "With what can we compare the kingdom of God, or what parable shall we use for it?" he said as the men and women in his audience leaned forward, intent on hearing his answer. "It is like a grain of mustard seed, which, when sown on the ground, is the smallest of all the seeds on earth, yet when it is sown it grows up and becomes larger than all the garden plants and puts out large branches, so that the birds of the air can make nests in its shade."[1] Some were visibly disappointed at the vague answer. Clearly some wanted the holy man to be plainer. Was he a revolutionary or not?

GODLY REVOLUTION

Lines of evidence converge suggesting that revolution was in the air when Yeshua spoke on Galilean hilltops and in Judean squares. Revolution did come forty years after Yeshua was taken up to the Father. The seeds of revolution had been there all along, ever since the Romans started their rule over Israel in 63 B.C.E.[2]

The prophets certainly used warrior themes as they described the age to come. "Then ADONAI will go out and fight against those nations, fighting as on a day of battle," said Zechariah.[3] One of the oldest prophecies said:

> I see him, but not now;
> I behold him, but not near:
> a star shall come out of Jacob,
> and a scepter shall rise out of Israel;
> it shall crush the forehead of Moab
> and break down all the sons of Sheth.
> Edom shall be dispossessed;
> Seir also, his enemies, shall be dispossessed.
> Israel is doing valiantly.[4]

To an Israelite in Yeshua's time, the time seemed long overdue for the scepter to rise out of Israel and crush the forehead of Moab, also known as Rome.

When the revolution did begin, there is evidence that it was fueled by religious fervor. Revolutionary zealots like those who died at Masada mixed religion with their warfare. The rebels against Rome found fuel for their fire in prophecies like Daniel 2. Josephus, the Jewish historian who tried to balance a pro-Roman view of destiny with loyalty to his Jewish heritage, carefully avoided the true message of Daniel. In his retelling of the story, Josephus avoided any implication that Daniel had foreseen doom for the Roman empire. If anything, Josephus' avoidance of the obvious is evidence that Daniel 2 was a popular text used in the call for revolt against Rome.[5]

The vision of Daniel 2 describes a final layer of a great statue—feet of mixed iron and clay. Josephus creatively alters some details so the feet of iron and clay will not seem so obvious a reference to the kingdom of Rome. Apparently Daniel 2 was interpreted during the Jewish Revolt as a sign that Israel would be the stone that crushed the feet of Rome and toppled the kingdoms of men.[6] Apparently there were those in Israel who believed Israel was about to become the kingdom that never ends.

YESHUA SUBVERTS THE PLOT

What did Yeshua make of this revolutionary talk? N.T. Wright captures the essence of the matter when he says Yeshua was retelling the "familiar story" of the kingdom Israel expected "in such a way as to subvert and redirect its normal plot."[7] To help us understand how Yeshua's retelling worked, we should look first at two other retellings: the Essene and the Josephus versions of the story.

The Essenes were the ultimate holy men, separated from any dealings with the unclean Israelites around them. They refused to participate in the Temple worship, though they believed in the Torah of Moses. The Temple was so corrupt to them; it was as if there was no Temple. A day would soon come when a Messianic priest arose and inaugurated a new Temple system. The Essenes would be the only elect and the rest of Israel would be judged with the nations as idolaters.[8] For the Essenes, the kingdom was limited to their own narrow sect. They were the counterpart of numerous groups today who believe their sect alone has the truth and that the entire world is doomed.

Josephus had a very different retelling of the expected kingdom story and Israel. Josephus had been a leader in the Jewish Revolt, but he surrendered himself to the Romans and became useful to them. He tried to discourage his countrymen from revolt and encourage them to accept Rome as God's protectors. He may have regarded Vespasian as the Messiah, the king who would bring peace for Israel. Josephus' retelling held that a pagan king was the one who would break all other kingdoms and bring peace.[9] The kingdom for Josephus was Rome.

So, we should not be surprised that Yeshua's teaching about the kingdom was a retelling also. Yeshua did not plan to take up arms against Rome. "Are you the King of the Jews?" Pilate asked. Yeshua's answer was, "My kingdom is not of this world."[10] "If someone hits you on one cheek, offer the other too; if someone takes your coat, let him have your shirt as well," Yeshua taught.[11] His reference was directly to the issue of revolution. Israel deserved Rome. Israel had fallen away from God. Israel was in exile. Only God would bring Israel out. The answer was not revolution.

"Repent, for the kingdom of heaven is at hand," was Yeshua's main message.[12] It was the good news, the gospel of the kingdom. Not revolution, repentance. Make repentance, not war. Look to God and wait for him. Do not try to bring the kingdom of heaven. It has begun in me, Yeshua said.

SUBVERTING OUR VIEW OF HEAVEN

Just as Israel had wrong ideas about the coming age, the kingdom of God, many have wrong ideas about heaven still: "I pray. I try to be kind to strangers and fellow drivers on the highways. I send money to disaster victims. I know God will let me in." There are other distorted views: "I am in the right denomination." Or, "imagine there's no heaven; it's easy if you try." Or, "the only heaven is what we make with our hands and our minds." Or, "heaven is for the great saints." Or, "I'd rather be with my friends in hell."

Yeshua's subversive message was not only a corrective to his own generation, but ours. "I tell you, many will come from east and west and recline at table with Abraham, Isaac, and Jacob in the kingdom of heaven, while the sons of the kingdom will be thrown into the outer darkness."[13] Some who expect to be there will not be.

"From the days of John the Baptist until now the kingdom of heaven has suffered violence, and the violent take it by force."[14] The kingdom is not something we can build by human ingenuity, improvement, or evolution.

"I tell you that unless you change and become like little children, you won't even enter the Kingdom of Heaven!"[15] It's not about sophistication. It's about simple trust.

"How blessed are those who make peace! for they will be called sons of God."[16] People who really want to be God's children must work as God does for Tikkun Olam, the repair of the world.

"For in the Resurrection, neither men nor women will marry; rather, they will be like angels in heaven."[17] Some of our greatest earthly joys will not exist when the kingdom of God comes. It follows that our earthly joys foreshadow a different kind of joy, something better.

Yeshua said little about what the World to Come would be like. He gave some hints. The poor in spirit, that is, the downtrodden, will own the kingdom of God. Mourners will be comforted there. The meek, who are last in this world, will inherit the land. Those who hunger for true goodness now will find it then.[18]

Most importantly, Yeshua tells us it will be full of the unexpected. If you listen to the wisdom of our master, you will see that we are out of our depth. We can neither bring the kingdom nor describe what it will be like. Many things will be turned around and the bottom will be the top. Much that is valued in human society will be of no value then.

The religious people surrounding Yeshua had their theories and even their certainties. God works in unexpected ways, Yeshua tells us. He calls us to be children. He invites people from far away to his banquet. He demands repentance, not revolution. He sends a martyr instead of a warrior. The kingdom of God is nothing if it is not a mystery.

GOSPEL, KINGDOM, AND TIKKUN OLAM

Our modern word, gospel, comes from a Greek word meaning a message of good news carried by a runner. For example, in ancient times, a city might be afraid of an approaching army. Imagine their relief and celebration when a runner would come to the gates to announce that the invading army was defeated and the city was safe.

Yeshua went throughout the land proclaiming an even better gospel. For the Messiah, the good news that God has for this world is far more than forgiveness for sin. Yeshua's gospel encompasses that and more:

> The time has come, God's Kingdom is near!
> Turn to God from your sins and believe the Good News![19]

God's kingdom does not refer to heaven or the afterlife. God's kingdom is his rule. Yeshua's message was simple: God's kingdom is coming soon and you are not ready.

The opposite of God's kingdom is the rule of man, the systems of government that dominate this present world order. Because the world is broken, the rule of man is characterized by oppression, injustice, and violence. God's rule is what will take this present world and change it into the World to Come.

Yeshua expected his hearers to start living under God's rule now and not to wait until that glorious future. Yeshua called on his generation to repent, to turn from their sins. Like the prophets of Israel, Yeshua had in mind the sins of injustice, greed, and self-serving religion. Yeshua's vision for a righteous man or woman was someone engaged in Tikkun Olam, bringing some of the World to Come into this world. That's why Yeshua spoke of comforting mourners, being peacemakers, clothing the naked, and visiting the sick.

For Yeshua, and so it should be for us, the gospel was not about benefits to be accrued in the future. The gospel is about God's rule beginning with us. The gospel is about being, not just receiving. The gospel is about being kingdom people.

BEING KINGDOM PEOPLE

Revolutionaries were plotting. The disciples of Shammai, an extremist group of Pharisees, had their own plots to purify Israel, ridding the land of heretics and Gentiles.[20] The Essenes were protesting and waiting for a day of God-ordained massacre to slaughter all but the sons of light, as they called themselves. The majority of those in Israel believed that being children of Abraham was sufficient. They would be included in the Age to Come by virtue of being born as Israelites.

Yeshua said only a few things here and there about what the World to Come would be like. He spent more time overthrowing the common answers about how to be included. He discomforted the comfortable and comforted the mourners.

Even his own disciples needed to have their expectations unsettled a bit. They followed him as Messiah, not just the twelve, but also many others who saw him pass through their Galilean towns. To them Yeshua said, "Not everyone who says to me, 'Lord, Lord,' will enter the kingdom of heaven."[21]

The common wisdom was that the righteous tended to be successful and materially blessed. While Yeshua did not avoid the wealthy and perhaps counted several among his broader group of disciples, he undermined such human reasoning. The citizens of the kingdom would be the poor in spirit, the meek, and the persecuted.[22]

In one of the few stories Yeshua told that pictures the afterlife, we read about a rich man who for years ignored a poor man who begged at his gates. The ignored beggar died and was carried by the angels of heaven to a better place. The rich man was buried, but no angels carried him. He awoke in a place of torment.[23] It would be a reversal. God's criteria for greatness radically differ from man's criteria. The beggar who appears most worthless might be one of God's holy ones.

So much of Yeshua's teaching was about reversal and the unexpected in the World to Come. The ones who are first here will often be last there.[24] Perhaps his most pointed teaching came when he found greater faith in a Roman centurion than in his fellow Israelites. Yeshua said there would be a banquet in the Age to Come. Many would come from far away, from the East and the West, and would find a seat at the great banquet table of the World to Come. Yet many of the sons of the kingdom, that is those in Israel to whom the kingdom should have been a natural concept, would find themselves excluded and cut off.[25]

While he may have said little about what the World to Come would be like, he said much about how to have a share in it. The masses that followed him and called him Lord had not yet found their way. He warned them to do the will of his father and to know and be known by him. Many others would seek after power or miracles, but he will say to them, "I never knew you."[26]

At the end, when the Son of Man comes to separate the nations, sending some to the eternal fire and others to the kingdom prepared before the foundation of the world, the difference would be deeds. The ones who did works of love, deeds of Tikkun Olam, such as caring for the sick, prisoners, and those needing clothes, they will find that they really were feeding and clothing Messiah.[27] It is just like the verse in Proverbs, that those who give to the poor lend to Adonai.[28]

Arguing about who would be greatest in the World to Come, the disciples were chastised by their master. Become like the children who followed him with simple adoration, Yeshua taught them.[29] Childlike faith is true greatness.

In John, the master puts it simply, "I have come as a light into the world, so that everyone who trusts in me might not remain in the dark."[30] Yeshua taught that the kingdom is dawning and the hour is late. The master will return like a thief. The World to Come that seems so distant is nearer than we think.

Our focus ought to be on being. We must be people of the kingdom. Simple trust and faith lead to changed hearts, which leads in turn to deeds of love and grace. The faithful, those full of faith, will not merely call Yeshua Lord, but will follow after him.

The kingdom does not come by violence. The kingdom does not come by success or self-importance. Rather, the kingdom is more greatly to be desired than a field full of treasure or a wealth of pearls. It is so great that giving up all in its service would be no sacrifice at all.

It is not that sacrifice is the way to the kingdom either. The way is Yeshua. The way is childlike trust. The way is doing the will of Yeshua's father. It comes naturally to those who believe and do not remain in darkness. They will be carried by angels to a better place. Theirs is the kingdom of God.

CHAPTER 6

The Vision of John

The ruins near Selcuk, Turkey are among the most impressive classical remains in the world. Here lie the ancient ruins of Ephesus. You can still see the temple of Domitian, the Gate of Heracles, and the temple of Goddess Rome and the Divine Caesar. Ephesus was one of the largest cities in the Roman Empire. It was not a place friendly to Christians.

According to some historical sources, the apostle John, one of the twelve, finished out his years in Ephesus.[1] It is one of the seven cities in Revelation.

The cultural background of Revelation is strewn with temples to the gods of Rome and the genius of Rome's caesars. Such cults of royalty and worship of military power were signs of the end, the hubris of man. Love not the world, John said in another of his books, nor the things of the world.[2]

The Christians in places like Ephesus had identity problems. They were no longer able to fit into Roman society as well as before. They could not show public obeisance to the gods of Rome or to its caesars. They came to be known as atheists for this reason.

At first, they sort of fit into the category of Jews. Many of them had been God-fearers, non-Jews who attended and participated in the synagogues.[3] Their God was the God of Israel. Their savior was the Messiah of Israel. Yet, more and more, the synagogue rejected them. More and more they were exposed to the Roman authorities as practicing illegal religion. They didn't belong to Judaism, a religion authorized by Rome as an exception or a *religio licita*.[4] If they weren't Jews and they weren't Romans, who were they? Where did they fit into God's plan for the ages?

This isn't just a question for them. It is a question for any follower of Yeshua today who is of the nations and not of Israel. Once the people of God had been almost exclusively Israelites. A few from

the nations would join with Israel. There were the occasional Naa-
mans and Ruths. But it was mostly Israel. So the prophets of Israel
looked at the coming of Messianic days from the vantage point of
Jerusalem and Israel. The nations were included, to be sure, but not
exactly at the center.

Where is a non-Jew to locate himself or herself in this Jewish
Bible of ours? This is one of the reasons that Revelation is such a
precious book, a treasure and needed desperately in the canon of
the Bible.

John adapts and expands on what the prophets said before him.
The community he serves is mostly non-Jewish. So in his vision the
nations are more at the center. Israel and the Jerusalem perspective
are not absent, but the full inclusion of the nations is more evident.

Also, John's community is suffering.[5] This may be why John's vision is largely about a time of great suffering. Revelation is a close-up
of suffering and persecution, which will occur during a seven-year
period called the tribulation. The concept first appears in Daniel 9,
a week of years that remains unaccounted for. John fills in the horrible gaps.

The seven-year tribulation is divided into two parts: A time, times,
and half a time—a way of saying three and a half years, or 1,260 days
or 42 months—other ways of saying three and a half years.

You could say that John was intent on using the number sev-
en—seven spirits before God's throne; seven menorahs (a.k.a. lamp
stands); seven stars in Yeshua's hand: seven seals; seven trumpets;
seven bowls; seven angels with seven plagues. There are even sev-
en symbolic figures in a sort of interlude section of Revelation: the
woman, the dragon, the male child, the angel Michael, the first and
second beast, and the Lamb.

There is a good hint that the plagues and tribulations of Revelation last exactly seven years. In chapter 12, God protects the woman,
Israel, for three and a half years.[6] Yet in Revelation 11, we see that
the holy city, Jerusalem, will be trampled by the nations for forty-two
months—three and a half years.[7] If these are two periods of time
back to back, they make seven years. The first half is a time of safety
for Israel. The second half is mayhem.

These might be called the Tribulation and the Great Tribulation.
John's persecuted community would want to know about God's

judgments on the corrupt power-kingdoms of the world, the kings of the earth who persecute, behead, and destroy.

In the larger view, Revelation is mostly about the bad news. The good stuff comes at the end. It is only in the last two chapters that paradise fully arrives, the New Jerusalem. John's suffering community reads about a time of suffering to come. They learn that suffering has an answer and dictators and empires fall.

THE HEAVENLY TEMPLE IN REVELATION

It's easy to overlook the Jewish themes in Revelation. In contrast to the prophets whose visions were very Israel-centered, Revelation is about all the nations. John assumed his readers knew the Hebrew scriptures and accepted as a matter of course Israel's centrality in future events. He wrote a book for the growing community of non-Jews following Yeshua. Yet his vision of things to come is still considerably Jewish.

Time has distorted most people's perspective on the World to Come. The last thing many people would expect to see in the future life is a temple like the old one in Jerusalem. And truly a day is coming when there will be no temple, says Revelation 21:22. Yet when Messiah comes, the Temple will stand for a millennium and there will be fire and stone, smoke and blood.

The Temple has been gone for two thousand years. Or has it?

John's visions from the little island of Patmos often bring him into the heavenly places to see images of God's throne. A pattern emerges in John's visions of the throne of the Holy One. God is not sitting in a field of heavenly wheat, nor in a crystal palace, but in a temple. It is a heavenly temple much like the earthly one.

If you were from Asia Minor, in the churches John served, you would not likely have ever seen the Temple. If many scholars are right about the time that Revelation was written, the Temple had been gone for twenty-five years.

Yet the idea of a heavenly temple was no surprise to John's readers. It was a part of their understanding of the cross. When Moses built the first sanctuary, he was to base it on a pattern.[8] The writer of

Hebrews had used this concept to discuss the superiority of Yeshua's sacrifice.[9]

Perhaps the surprise for many modern readers is the idea that God hasn't moved on. In the minds of many, things like temples are primitive. Surely by the time John wrote Revelation, God would have given up old ideas. Wouldn't God want to prepare his new world-wide community for more advanced ideas of worship?

"I turned around to see who was speaking to me; and when I had turned, I saw seven gold menorahs," says John in Revelation 1:12. Many modern readers might miss that these are menorahs, since the translations usually say lamp stands. The menorah, the seven-branched light in the Temple, was a lamp stand.

It's easy to miss the heavenly temple scenery in Revelation if you don't know what to look for. You might miss Yeshua's priestly robe in 1:13, where he is depicted as the priest maintaining the lights of the seven congregations. You might miss the possibility that the twenty-four elders in 4:4 could represent the twenty-four courses of the priesthood from 1 Chronicles 24:4. You may not see that the "sea of glass" in 4:6 is the basin from the Temple.[10] When incense is burned in 5:8 and the censer and altar of incense are used in 8:3, you have to know the Temple to understand it. In 11:19, John just comes right out and says it, "Then the Temple of God in heaven was opened, and the Ark of the Covenant was seen in his Temple; and there were flashes of lightning, voices, peals of thunder, an earthquake and violent hail."

The Temple of God in Jerusalem was an earthly picture of heavenly majesty and transcendent holiness. It was a true picture then and will be in the Messianic Age, when it becomes the throne of the Lord on earth, as it is now the throne of God in heaven.

And in other ways too, Revelation has not lost the Israel perspective.

ISRAEL AND THE JERUSALEM PERSPECTIVE IN REVELATION

In more ways than one John's apocalyptic visions keep Israel at the center. Jerusalem is still the stage. We learn in Revelation 12 what great motive of the evil one is behind so much suffering: his desire to destroy Israel. We learn in Revelation 7 and 14 about a vanguard of Israel, 12,000 from each tribe, who play a major role in climactic events. Though some try, it's a strain to interpret these 144,000 as anything other than Jews, since their tribal affiliations are specifically revealed. But, more importantly, there is a drama in Revelation 11 that really shows how Israel's story impacts the world's story.

Is the seed of Abraham really such a central piece of the World to Come? Some would just assume that since most of Israel rejected Messiah, God has moved on. Yet, Israel's restoration is the turning point in the world's restoration. Yeshua once said to Jerusalem, "For I tell you, from now on, you will not see me again until you say, 'Blessed is he who comes in the name of ADONAI.'"[11] Jerusalem's turning is the crux of history. Jerusalem's turning is what Yeshua is waiting for.

Revelation 11 lifts the curtain and shows us the drama. The scene is the holy city, Jerusalem. John, like the angelic being in Ezekiel 40, is measuring the Temple in Jerusalem. He is told not to measure the court of the Gentiles. This is all a sign, his heavenly guide explains, that Jerusalem is to be trampled on by Gentiles for three and a half years.

Enter into the drama the story of the two witnesses. They speak to the world from Jerusalem. Anti-Messiah, the Beast, kills them. And then they are raised from the dead and called up into the heavens, like Elijah.

At the time of their resurrection, there is an earthquake. One tenth of Jerusalem is destroyed and 7,000 are killed.

Things look bad for Jerusalem. But then the defining moment happens: "[T]he rest were awestruck and gave glory to the God of heaven."[12] The people of Jerusalem awaken. The people in the city of God return to God. At last, Jerusalem gives glory to the God who founded the city.

And, just as the prophets said and Yeshua said, this is the turning point. Right afterwards, we get the best news in the history of the world: "The kingdom of the world has become the Kingdom of our Lord and his Messiah, and he will rule forever and ever!"[13]

Revelation confirms what we have read in the prophets. Jerusalem will be a liability to the rest of the world, says Zechariah 12. Jerusalem will be attacked and persecuted. But suddenly grace will be poured out on Jerusalem. "They will call on my name and I will answer them," said Zechariah.[14] They will see the pierced one and mourn and their troubles will be turned to joy.

Israel's joy means joy for the whole world.

THE NATIONS, THE MULTITUDE, AND THE MARTYRS

God's plan is and always has been to make something perfect out of this world and all mankind. Israel has always been the center of something bigger than Israel. Revelation takes God's program for Israel, from the prophets of Israel, and transforms it into God's program for the world.

The Yeshua movement grew rapidly among non-Jews. Greeks and Romans were reading Israel's scriptures. It must have been hard for them to find their place in the scriptures. Some turned to a theology of supersessionism or replacement. More and more Israel was read out of the scriptures. Christians put themselves in Israel's place.

There was no need. The vision has always been humanity-wide. Revelation beautifully transitions a Jewish hope into a humanity-wide hope.

Right after the 144,000 are introduced, a corresponding group is revealed. They are a multitude. They are uncountable. They are like sand. They are clothed in white robes and have palm branches in their hands.[15]

Where did John get a picture of Gentiles wearing white and carrying palm branches? He got it from Zechariah 14:16. This prophetic passage says that in the days of Messiah, the nations will come to the Temple and celebrate Booths, also called Tabernacles or Sukkot.

Aren't these uncountable masses of Gentiles a little early? Messiah hasn't set up his kingdom yet. What are they doing celebrating the Feast before its time?

Remember: this is a vision. It has symbolic meaning. The symbolism is not difficult to discern. The prophets foretold a great mass of Gentiles worshipping Messiah at the Feast in the days of Messiah. John says they are already here.

Since the days the good news of Messiah first went out, the nations have been coming in. Romans 11:25 calls our time the fullness of the Gentiles. In ancient Turkey, Greece, Italy, and spreading even to China and America and Kenya, the mass has been growing. These are the righteous from the nations. They are called to the days of Messiah along with Israel.

John's vision provides a view that is humanity-wide. The days of Messiah and the New Jerusalem are for the whole earth. God's love came through Israel to spread to everyone.

And in a time of worldwide plague and suffering, John tells us how to get in on the great Feast to come.

THE TRIBULATION IN DETAIL

The prophets of Israel said there would be trouble before Messiah's redemption. They spoke of all the nations attacking Jerusalem. We call it Armageddon.

Daniel spoke of seventy weeks of years that were to play a role in Israel's future. He explained sixty-nine of those weeks, but left one mysterious. Revelation 6 through 19 at last fills in the details. It will not be a good time. But the faithful will endure to the end.

The story of the tribulation is told as a series of judgments initiated by the Lamb opening a scroll. The Lamb, Yeshua, is the only one worthy to open these judgments, since he died to rescue people from judgment. These judgments are directed at those who did not believe in his love. Meanwhile, the faithful who must endure them at least have hope at the end.

The judgments each begin with a scroll sealed at seven spots with sealing wax. The Lamb unrolls the scroll and breaks a seal. Each seal unleashes a new time of pain and destruction on the earth. The seventh seal becomes seven trumpets, seven more judgments added to the six already unleashed. The seventh trumpet becomes seven bowls, more judgments added to the twelve already begun.

The tribulation will be a time of famines and wars. It will be a time of martyrdom for Yeshua-followers. Men will hide in caves and beg mountains to fall on them. Political systems will be destroyed and new ones will rise. There will be signs in the heavens. Demonic powers will be released. Plagues like the ones in Exodus will fall on mankind. Babylon will fall, an image that could mean many different things.

And after all these horrible pains, when much of the world has been killed, when things are at their worst, he will come. He will come on a white horse.

THE ANOINTED CONQUEROR

Isaiah had already announced him, this anointed conqueror. He is anointed to announce good news to the poor and to release those in prison.[16] Once Yeshua read this scripture in the synagogue as Luke tells us in his fourth chapter. When Yeshua read it, a promise of one who would release the prisoners and proclaim good news to the poor, he said this scripture was speaking about him. Yet he stopped before the end of Isaiah 61:2. He didn't read the final part of the anointed conqueror's mission: to proclaim "the day of the vengeance of our God."[17]

If you follow along in Isaiah, the scripture goes on to say more about the anointed conqueror. He comes from Edom, from Bozrah, with bloodstained robes. He is red with the blood of God's enemies, of Jerusalem's enemies.[18] He has been treading a winepress, a terrible winepress of blood and not of grapes. He is the Messiah coming to avenge Israel and to slay God's enemies. He is Yeshua, not only the world's savior, but also the judge.

John describes this very scene in Revelation 19. Yeshua comes as the white rider with eyes of flame. Yeshua's robe is soaked in blood. He is called the Word, the logos, the memra.[19] The armies of heaven follow him. He strikes down the nations with the sword of his verbal power to command life and death. He is the King of Kings and Lord of Lords. Caesar and anti-Messiah are no more. The kingdom of this world has become the kingdom of our Lord and his Messiah. The Anointed Conqueror will come, riding on a white horse. He will carry out the day of vengeance of our God.

THE MILLENNIUM

John makes another unique contribution to our understanding of the World to Come. He informs us, in ways that cannot be discerned with clarity anywhere else in the Bible, that the World to Come arrives in two stages.

A similar view developed in later Judaism.[20] The days of Messiah are a transitional time between this world and the World to Come:

> How long will the days of Messiah last? R. Akiba said, Forty years, as long as the Israelites were in the wilderness ... R. Judah the prince said, Four hundred years, as long as the Israelites were in Egypt. R. Eliezer (b. Hyrcanus) said, A thousand years.[21]

John's answer is in Revelation 20, and it is a thousand years. It is a time when Satan is chained in the Abyss. The followers of Yeshua out of the tribulation come to life and reign with Messiah for the thousand years.[22] They will reign over the people who survived the tribulation but who were not followers of the King.

At the end of the thousand years, Satan will be let loose again. Many will follow his rebellion, surprisingly, and rebel against Yeshua on earth. John describes this as the fulfillment of Gog and Magog, the prophetic battle of Ezekiel 38–39. Fire from heaven ends the battle and Satan is cast into a lake of fire.

But why this transitional period? Why does there need to be a time of a thousand years before the World to Come is finally here?

First, this time is when God restores Israel and brings the kingdom of this world to its highest glory. This can only happen in an earthly kingdom.[23] Even when Messiah returns and the kingdom is on earth, God has work yet to do before he brings the perfection of all things.

Second, it may be that the days of Messiah are in a way God's proof that humankind is broken. There will be no devil to blame for sin during these years. The King will be visible and out in the open. People will see miracles. Humankind is full of excuses before God. We think we can say to God that our rebelliousness is not our fault. And yet, while Satan is chained and the King is out in the open, still very many will not believe.

All the excuses of non-believers crumble to dust in the millennium. But those who believe will see the city of God come down from heaven.

THE NEW JERUSALEM

"I saw the holy city, New Jerusalem, coming down out of heaven from God," says John.[24] Those who have seen the present Jerusalem often remark about its beauty. The stones look golden by the light of the setting or rising sun. Jerusalem of gold, people call it.

So the New Jerusalem follows the pattern of the World to Come. It is not something completely new and unconnected to our experience. The New is continuous in some ways with the Old. The beauty of the World to Come is a perfection of this world, not a wholly new world.

John knew the beauty of Jerusalem. God made him understand, all that beauty and splendor are a sign of better things to come. The New Jerusalem will be like the Old, only so much better. It is a New Heaven and Earth. It has the same things as this heaven and earth, only better.

CHAPTER 7

Hints of Heaven

The undying lands in the West. Avalon beyond the mists. The realm just beyond our grasp, as near as a touch but as far removed as life after death. Heaven is an idea that stirs the imagination.

In C. S. Lewis's *The Great Divorce*, heaven is a place much more substantial than earth. One of the citizens of heaven says:

All hell is smaller than one pebble of your earthly world: but it is really smaller than one atom of this world, the Real World. Look at yon butterfly. If it swallowed all Hell, Hell would not be big enough to do it any harm or have any taste.[1]

It is a land that goes on forever into the west. Upon arriving for a holiday in heaven, the main character gets a glimpse to the west:

But very far away I could see what might either be a great bank of cloud or a range of mountains. Sometimes I could make out in it steep forests, far-withdrawing valleys, and even mountain cities perched on inaccessible summits. At other times it became indistinct. The height was so enormous that my waking sight could not have taken in such an object at all. Light brooded on the top of it: slanting down thence it made long shadows behind every tree on the plain.[2]

The green hills roll ever on and on beneath a clear blue sky. Crystal streams trickle over soft brown stones decorated with verdant moss. Every image we have of a better land, a land of fantasy, light, goodness, and truth, is a possible image of the World to Come.

Is it safe to enter a forest there or to journey into the mountains? On earth there might be dangers in such beautiful places, but in the World to Come there are no perils any more. Could there be beauty without danger? Adventure without risk? Joy without pain? Here we cannot imagine such a thing, but there it will be reality.

This present world is a world that smothers the heart. In our hearts we long for beauty, truth, and lasting joy. Yet in this world beauty is marred. Truth is veiled. Joy inevitably gets corrupted or destroyed. This present world teaches us to harden our hearts, not to expect too much joy. We live with heartache, try not to become black-hearted, and hope for more with all our hearts.[3]

Still, all that doesn't mean we don't feel. Our hearts face death, but stubbornly refuse to die all the way. We keep returning to the desires of the heart, never fulfilled but always there. This is not a feminine or a masculine thing. It is universal. Men and women desire to love and be loved, to triumph and know adventure and mystery. We call someone who lacks these desires heartless. But heartlessness is an illusion. No person is really heartless. The desire for adventure and beauty is universal, even among those who fight against it to live in cynicism.

Children long to conquer the high seas or play the hero. Girls desire a prince to come and woo them. Boys crave an adventure, a quest worthy of great courage. Some continue this longing in their experience of art, seeing an ideal world in a painting. Some continue it in stories or literature or movies. We all travel this world of the heart in our imagination, sometimes perverted but ideally pure, even holy.

C. S. Lewis found it in many places in imagination, nursery stories, poetry, and literature. In *Surprised By Joy*, he describes it:

It is . . . an unsatisfied desire, which is itself more desirable than any other satisfaction. I call it Joy, which here is a technical term and must be sharply distinguished from both Happiness and from Pleasure. Joy (in my sense) has indeed one characteristic, and only one, in common with them; the fact that anyone who has experienced it will want it again. Apart from that . . . it might also equally well be called a particular kind of unhappiness or grief. But then it is a kind we want. I doubt that anyone who has tasted it would ever, if both were in his power, exchange it for all the pleasures in the world. But then Joy is never in our power and pleasure often is.[4]

Joy is what men and women are seeking but can never find in cheap sex. It is what a beer and some friends might buy for a few moments, but which is not fully achieved. It is why we seek entertainment, to escape to Joy for a brief vacation of the soul.

Could Joy have anything to do with the hereafter? Did God leave some Joy in the world after the Garden was closed?

THE WAY GOD RESTORES

You could think of this present life as a sort of exile. In many ancient cultures a crime could get you exiled. The Romans were fond of this punishment for people of noble position who committed a crime. To be exiled is to be forbidden to return home. So we find ourselves in exile. Our home is paradise, but we are exiled to a lesser land. We find in ourselves a longing for our true home, like a Roman noble exiled to a foreign land.

Yet a Roman exiled to a place like Asia Minor would still find some Roman life there. Some foods would remind him of home. He might see some people traveling from Rome and long to be back where he belongs. In the same way, we get glimpses of our true home from this present exile.

In the Bible, the people of God were once exiled to Babylon. Maybe we can find in the Bible a hint of how God treats people when they leave exile and return home. Maybe we can get some idea of what awaits us at the end of our exile. Maybe we can see in Israel's story of exile and return some hint for our greater future. We get just such an opportunity in the book of Isaiah.

Isaiah was a court prophet during the 8th century B.C.E. He was alive during the awful time when Assyria came and crushed the northern tribes of Israel. Yet down in the south, where Isaiah lived, the kingdom of Judah survived. Yet it was revealed to Isaiah that Judah was headed for its own disaster.

The disaster would not come for a little over a century after Isaiah's lifetime. Being a prophet, however, God gave Isaiah messages for the future. The prophet delivered God's words warning people of a coming exile. It would be a time of unimaginable horror. Yet God also gave Isaiah a positive message for the time after the exile was over. Isaiah wrote prophecies specifically for people who would not be born for two centuries.

Many scholars have trouble believing Isaiah wrote the entire book attributed to him. It seems odd that God would give a prophet messages specifically for generations as yet unborn. Starting in Isaiah 40, that is exactly what we have, an 8th century prophet speaking to 6th century people.

COMFORT, COMFORT MY PEOPLE

The first words of Isaiah to the people coming out of exile are, "Comfort, comfort my people, says your God."[5] God is no longer punishing or casting Israel into exile, "Speak tenderly to Jerusalem, and cry to her that her warfare is ended, that her iniquity is pardoned."[6]

When God's people come out of exile, his way is comfort. God offers consolation from grief and anxiety. God offers to heal the heart. The exile is over and the heart should be allowed to heal.

Isaiah 40 continues and speaks of a people brought back to freedom, released from exile. The prophecy paints a picture of a new relationship between Israel and the God of Israel: "He will tend his flock like a shepherd; he will gather the lambs in his arms; he will carry them in his bosom, and gently lead those that are with young."[7]

Imagine a painting with rolling hills dotted with flocks. This is a familiar scene in the Middle East. The shepherd is there and the sheep are his life. He carries one lamb against his bosom. The bosom is located at the heart. To be held in the bosom is to be close to the heart. God promises to hold Israel close to his heart. Imagine God as your shepherd and ask what joy could be greater.

Meanwhile, down here in exile-land, we are tired. We doubt. We survive in a heartless land. But, again speaking to Israel coming out of exile, God has a promise: ". . . those who hope in Adonai will renew their strength, they will soar aloft as with eagles' wings; when they are running they won't grow weary, when they are walking they won't get tired."[8]

All the heartaches will be removed. Our spirits will be renewed. God heals the hearts of his returnees. Here, in the present earth, the heart faints. In the World to Come, the heart will be restored. "Delight yourself in [Adonai] and he will give you the desires of your heart."[9]

A TEXT ALONGSIDE THE BIBLE

The Bible does not tell us everything about the World to Come. Yet it tells us enough to know more than what it says. From the Bible we determine that there is another text, one that lies alongside the Bible and prefigures the World to Come.

The desires of the heart point the way. The unsatisfied desire will at last be satisfied. Joy will be real.

A family enjoys a day hike in the clear mountain air. It is a sign. A woman enjoys a story of love found at last. It is a sign. A child looks longingly at a picture in a storybook. It is a sign.

We can experience signs every day, though we easily overlook them. We can be reminded a thousand times what the World to Come may be like. It is there in beauty. We can simply look at the face of our spouse and see a hint of heaven. We can curl our toes in green grass and know paradise is real. We hear a child's innocent laughter and we can imagine. We forget ourselves and fall into the joy of friends and conversation. We can imagine true companionship that will never end or lead to disappointment.

Just as John saw at the end of Revelation, the New Jerusalem comes down over the old. The new earth is both like and unlike this present earth. The love, laughter, and light we desire here is the reality of the World to Come.

God has given us more information about the World to Come than we might think. Artists seek to capture it sometimes in paintings. Writers try to evoke a sense of it when describing fantastic lands. We know about the World to Come because of desire, the deepest desires of our heart. God has truly written eternity on our hearts, as the Preacher in Ecclesiastes said long ago.[10]

CHAPTER 8

The Horrors of Hell

H ell. "Abandon all hope, ye who enter here," said the sign in Dante's *Inferno*. The biblical image varies between descriptions of fire and utter darkness. Hell is a horrible place to contemplate. Yet no picture of the World to Come is complete without considering the reality of the place of judgment.

Hell is a topic rife with myth and misunderstanding. The devil with his pitchfork supposedly rules here. The Bible does not promote this myth at all, but says rather, "The Adversary who had deceived them was hurled into the lake of fire and sulfur, where the beast and the false prophet were; and they will be tormented day and night forever and ever."[1] It doesn't sound like he'll be doing much ruling. Hell, says Yeshua, was created for the devil and his angels as a place of judgment for them.[2]

Hell is also a topic that raises questions. In his book, *The Case for Faith*, Lee Strobel interviewed Charles Templeton, a former evangelist turned atheist. Templeton bitterly argued against God by trying to show that God is not good:

I couldn't hold someone's hand to a fire for a moment. Not an instant! How could a loving God, just because you don't obey him and do what he wants, torture you forever — not allowing you to die, but to continue in that pain for eternity? There is no criminal who would do this![3]

Indeed, hell seems a place out of character for God. Just what is this place and what is it like?

THE BASIC BIBLICAL PICTURE

If you try to find the Bible's teaching on hell, you can easily be led astray. Don't use a concordance to search for the word. Some translations of the Bible use the word hell where only the grave is meant, the Hebrew *sheol*.

If by hell we mean a place of judgment after this life, then we only see this concept in one or two places in the Hebrew scriptures. The first is less than certain and it comes at the end of Isaiah. As Isaiah sees the time when God will perfect the world, he sees two groups. One group trembles at God's word.[4] The other group chooses their own way, even though they are religious.[5] It's interesting that the first group consigned to judgment in the Bible are religious hypocrites!

Isaiah's prophecy, rather difficult to understand, goes on with a contrast between the blessedness of the first group and the doom of the second. At the end, the blessed group goes out to look on the dead bodies of the doomed. Isaiah says, "For their worm will never die, and their fire will never be quenched; but they will be abhorrent to all humanity."[6] Later, Yeshua himself uses this imagery to describe hell.[7]

The second place in the Hebrew scriptures that describes a place of judgment after this life is far more certain. In Daniel 12:2, we read again of two groups. Both groups are raised to life. Yet the first is raised to life while the second is raised to "shame and everlasting contempt." It is significant that the first idea of hell being everlasting is from the Hebrew scriptures.

When we turn to the New Testament, what sort of picture do we get of hell? We find that Yeshua, Paul, and other New Testament teachers speak of a time of judgment after this life. Yeshua puts it unequivocally in one place: "They will go off to eternal punishment, but those who have done what God wants will go to eternal life."[8]

As Christopher Morgan puts it in *Hell Under Fire*, there are three aspects to the New Testament picture of hell: punishment, destruction, and banishment.[9]

The punishment aspect of hell is very common and can be found in scriptures such as: Mark 9:42-48; Matthew 5:20-30; Luke 16:19-31; 2 Thessalonians 1:5-10; Hebrews 10:27-31; James 5:1-5; 2 Peter 2:4-17; Jude 13-23; and Revelation 20:10-15.

The theme of hell as destruction might incline us to believe that hell is not eternal punishment. If the doomed are destroyed, then they will not exist any longer, right? Yet the picture of destruction was seen by biblical authors in harmony with hell as suffering. Something can continue to exist in a destroyed state. References to hell as destruction include: Matthew 7:13-14, 24-27; Luke 13:3-5; John 3:16; Romans 9:22; Galatians 6:8; 1 Thessalonians 5:13; 1 Timothy 6:9; Hebrews 10:27; James 5:20; 2 Peter 2:6; and Revelation 21:8.

Finally, hell is also banishment from the presence of God. References include: Matthew 7:21-23; 8:12; 13:42, 50; 25:10-12; Luke 16:19-31; 2 Thessalonians 1:5-10; and Revelation 22:14-15.

Aside from punishment, destruction, and banishment, what is hell like? The Bible uses two primary images. The first and best known is fire. Yeshua calls it the eternal fire in Matthew 25:41 and speaks of fire that will never be quenched in Mark 9:48. The second and lesser-known image is darkness. Yeshua speaks of some being cast into the outer darkness where there is gnashing of teeth in Matthew 8:12; 22:13; 25:30.

It is evident from these varying descriptions, fire and darkness, that hell is being described in images. Is hell truly a place of continual immolation in fire? We cannot say, but we know that images often communicate something different than the image. You would not find fire and darkness in the same place here on earth, so perhaps we should not be so literal about the fire in hell. We can take literally, however, the ideas of hell as punishment, destruction, and banishment.

But what of God's love? Can this really be his plan? Such questions have led people to some alternative theories.

SOME ALTERNATIVE THEORIES

Annihilationism is the theory that when people die who are not included in the World to Come, they cease to exist. In some versions the wicked may suffer briefly before going out of existence. The basis of this theory is three-fold: (1) It does not seem right for God to punish people for eternity, (2) the scriptures speak of hell as destruction, (3) and the idea that all souls live for eternity is a Greek idea and foreign to the Bible.

There are some solid arguments for annihilationism. Michael Green asserts that the "eternal" in eternal life as well as in eternal punishment is not really about length of time but about the quality or finality of that life or punishment.[10] This argument has some merit and perhaps someday we will find it is true. Yet the destiny of the righteous and the wicked is always shown in parallel. If the righteous have joy forever, it seems the scriptural writers are saying the wicked have punishment forever. Furthermore, the scriptural concept of banishment, seen in passages like Revelation 22:15, suggests that life does not cease to exist for the wicked.

Another alternative theory is universalism, the idea that eventually all will be saved. C. S. Lewis presented in a favorable light the theory of George MacDonald. When asked if those in hell may find a way out into heaven, the character of George MacDonald replies:

> If they leave that grey town behind it will not have been hell. To any that leaves it, it is Purgatory . . . but to those who remain there, it will have been Hell even from the beginning. . . . ye cannot in your present state understand eternity . . . but ye can get some likeness of it if ye say that both good and evil, when they are full grown, become retrospective. Not only this valley but also all this earthly past will have been Heaven to those who are saved . . . Heaven, once obtained, will work backwards and turn even that agony into a glory.[11]

The ultimate fate of the wicked is left a mystery in Lewis's version, but there is hope that after a long time, all the citizens of hell might make it to heaven.

There is a similar view in rabbinic literature:

> There are three classes with regard to the Day of Judgment: the perfectly righteous, the completely wicked, and the average people. Those in the first class are forthwith inscribed and sealed for eternal life. Those in the second-class are forthwith inscribed and sealed for Gehinnom [hell]. . . . The third will descend to Gehinnom and cry out . . . and then ascend.[12]

The rabbinic view does not say that all will eventually be saved, but indicates that many who do not make it into the World to Come at first will do so after spending some time in hell. For the rabbis, the longest anyone would spend in hell was twelve months. Once Rabbi Yochanan ben Zakkai, however, did indicate a belief in eternal punishment.[13]

Will it be that after some time, God will redeem all, even the most wicked? Could hell be temporary for most or all people?

Again, terms like everlasting punishment and eternal destruction in the scriptures would seem to argue against universalism.

Finally, there is a view that I will call separationism. It is the idea that hell will not be so bad, but will mainly consist of being separated from God's presence. It rejects the idea of agony and torment.

This is the hopeful view indicated in C. S. Lewis's *The Great Divorce*. The citizens of hell live in a grey, murky town. They live in perpetual twilight. There seems to be no purpose to life. Yet they are not in flames or any torment other than the inner torment of meaningless existence.

Christian philosopher, J. P. Moreland, also seems to advocate such a theory in an interview by Lee Strobel in *The Case for Faith*:

Remember, it's not torture. . . . The wording is critical. It's not eternal conscious torture; it's eternal conscious suffering due to being sentenced away from God.[14]

Moreland explains that fire and darkness are not literal, since these images cancel each other out. The flame imagery is symbolic of God's judgment. The image of worms that never die is a case of Yeshua using the literal valley of Gehinnom outside Jerusalem as a metaphor for hell. The famous gnashing of teeth is about people being angry when they realize they've been shut out.[15]

Separationism downplays the physical torment images of hell for a friendlier version that is easier for us to bear thinking about. While it is hopeful, we should remember that the biblical picture of hell is not only banishment, but also destruction and punishment. Maybe hell is truly not the feeling of being burned alive for eternity, but perhaps it is worse than living in perpetual twilight.

These alternative theories (annihilationism, universalism, and separationism) could have some elements of truth to them. It is possible that God has revealed only a part of the total picture of hell. Perhaps we will later learn that the images we took for eternal conscious torment were not the full picture.

Still, this side of the life to come, we cannot put our hope in such theories. We have to be prepared for the fact that standing before the Living God in judgment is more unpleasant than any earthly experience. While we may be hopeful for our loved ones that hell is not a complete torment, we do well to fear the judgment of God. The Bible does not give us a clear basis for an optimistic view of eternal judgment.

RIGHTNESS IN HIS JUDGMENT

For those who respect the judgment of God as absolute and who tremble at God's word, is there any hope that hell might not be so infernal? Does the doctrine of hell make God an eternal torturer? What of ordinary unbelievers, whose sins seem mild to us?

We do know from scripture that God does not judge all people with the same level of punishment. Yeshua said more than once of the towns that saw his miracles and rejected them, "It will be more tolerable on the day of judgment for the land of Sodom than for you."[16] Yeshua also spoke of weightier and lesser issues of the law.[17]

Perhaps, then, we can hope that our loved ones who did not appear to us to be saved, might not be suffering nearly as much as the worst texts about punishment describe. Perhaps also, we will find that our understanding of hell from the Bible was limited. From the limited revelation that God has given us, and from our limited perspective in time, perhaps we do not fully understand. But regardless of all the maybes, we do know one comforting thing for sure. We know that there is rightness in God's judgment.

It is a great mistake to imagine that the God who speaks so beautifully in scripture and whose love is demonstrated so beautifully by the sacrificial death of the Son of God would be less than good in judging those who end up excluded. God is perfect in his love. No one will stand before him and be able to find fault in the rightness of his judgment.

As George MacDonald's character said to the protagonist in *The Great Divorce*, "Ye can know nothing of the end of all things . . . because all answers deceive."[18] Hell remains something of a mystery, though we learn it is banishment, punishment, and destruction. What we must do now is trust in the rightness of God's judgment and do what we can to keep ourselves and our loved ones from facing destruction.

CHAPTER 9

The Drama of the Coming Ages

Christendom has three basic outlines of the drama that is coming. All three dramatic outlines include the King and his subjects. The King, of course, is Yeshua, and the subjects are Christians. Yet the similarity of players belies the divergence of dramatic plots.

In one plot the subjects of the kingdom prepare a transitional kingdom for the King before he comes. After that, the King comes and completes the process already started by his subjects. He will put away all evil and make a world only of good after his subjects have prepared the way. There are diverse views about how the subjects will prepare the way for the King. Some see the subjects doing this through worldly power (politics) and others through spiritual means (evangelism). This view is called postmillennialism, with the word millennium meaning a thousand years. The importance of a thousand year period of time comes from Revelation 20:1–6.

In another plot, we are already in the transitional kingdom, but the kingdom is invisible. The King rules now over those who by faith believe he is the King. The subjects of the King are those who know now, when he is not present, that the King rules. The King will come and establish the Final Age without any earthly transition. All evil will be put away in one step. This view is called amillennialism because it takes the thousand years as figurative.

Finally, there is the view that the King will come and prepare a transitional kingdom for his subjects. It is not possible for the subjects to bring the Messianic Age and conquer sin, Satan, and the world before the King comes. Therefore it is up to the King to bring the transitional kingdom. That kingdom will last for a thousand years and there will be a final rebellion. After that, the King will establish the Final Age and put away all evil. This view is called premillennialism, because the King will come before the millennium.

These three dramatic plots are very different. One places a great deal of faith in the Church and human ability, empowered by the Spirit, to conquer evil and spread the influence of God on the earth. One is content to see many promises of the King's in a figurative manner, so that blessings are only for the faithful and are intangible. Only premillennialism views the promises as literal blessings in human time and story while at the same time insisting that only the King can bring them to pass.

Rabbinic Judaism has two basic views of the coming ages. In Judaism there are many variations, especially since the advent of the enlightenment and liberal Judaism, but I am speaking here of the views of the sages as indicated in rabbinic literature.[1]

The rabbis spoke of the World to Come as well as the Days of Messiah. Some saw them as the same: Messiah will bring the World to Come all in one step. Others saw them as different: Messiah will bring a transitional kingdom that will precede the World to Come.

The plot of the second rabbinic view is essentially the same as the Christian premillennial plot. The King will come and establish a transitional kingdom. Even the glory of that transitional kingdom, the millennium, the days of Messiah, the Age to Come, will greatly surpass the reality of the present age. Then, after the Messianic Age will come a final kingdom, the Olam Ha-Ba, the World to Come. Those days will surpass even the Messianic Age in glory and rejoicing.

THE END OF THIS AGE

The biblical drama of the coming ages involves several players: the King, who can be understood as God or Messiah; the subjects, who include Israel and the nations who have called on the name of Adonai; and the wicked of the nations who oppose the King and his kingdom, preferring to establish their own kingdoms in defiance of him; and the great masses, who do not choose to follow the King and are deceived.

There are several very interesting versions of the drama. We will consider some of the versions and see what they have in common: Daniel's unbreakable kingdom, Joel's valley of judgment, Zechariah's warrior God, Yeshua's fig tree, and John's scroll of judgments.

DANIEL'S UNBREAKABLE KINGDOM

Daniel's drama is in some ways the easiest to understand, and in some details the hardest. It helps knowing the setting of Daniel. Daniel's drama about the unbreakable kingdom fits his life. He saw the rise and fall of Babylon the Great. Daniel saw the drama in a series of great visions, all about the succeeding kingdoms of men that will one day be supplanted by the unbreakable kingdom.

Daniel was a faithful Jew living faithfully in the pagan kingdoms of Babylon and Persia. He had been taken away as a boy. He lost all he had but a few friends. His captors took him because he was one of the brightest and best. He was to be trained. He was to become a courtier in the royal house. He was to be assimilated into Persian ways.

Yet Daniel would not assimilate. He would not cease to be a Jew. He ate vegetables and turned away the fine food of the palace. He continued praying three times a day toward Jerusalem when it nearly cost him his life. He was an unbreakable Jew surviving unharmed through kingdom upheavals.

Daniel saw, through Nebuchednezzar, a statue of mixed media: gold, silver, bronze, iron, and iron mixed with clay.[2] Later, Daniel himself saw a succession of beasts: an eagle-winged lion, a bear, a four-headed, four-winged leopard, and a ten-horned beast with teeth of iron.[3] Each of these visions was a plot fitting for the life of Daniel: they represented the rising and falling of great human kingdoms.

In both of these visions, the rising and falling kingdoms of man are supplanted by an unbreakable kingdom. A stone not cut with human hands smashes the statue of mixed media:

In the days of those kings the God of heaven will establish a kingdom that will never be destroyed, and that kingdom will not pass into the hands of another people. It will break to pieces and consume all those kingdoms; but it, itself, will stand forever.[4]

A kingdom granted to one "like a son of man" by "the Ancient of Days" supplants the succession of terrible beasts.[5] The message is that kings will rise, but in the end, the "holy ones of the Most High" will "possess the kingdom forever."[6]

Daniel goes on to say more about the fourth beast, with ten horns and iron teeth. It is the most ferocious of all and devours the whole earth. One of the ten horns is different from the others, having eyes and a mouth. It speaks and makes war with the Holy Ones of Adonai. The ten horns are ten kings in succession in this terrible fourth kingdom. This last is the greatest and conquers the whole earth. He is the greatest king until the King of Kings comes down. He reigns until the Son of Man and the Holy Ones receive the kingdom from the Ancient of Days.[7]

JOEL'S VALLEY OF JUDGMENT

Joel's valley of judgment is more limited in scope, a simpler plot. Joel is a prophet we know almost nothing about. We can't even say when his book was written. Yet Joel delivered a series of messages from God that told a story. It is a fascinating story to piece together.

Hard times are coming for Judah and Jerusalem. The Day of Adonai is coming, a day of terrible judgment. Joel's foreboding descriptions prepare us for the later graphic detail of Revelation. A series of judgments falls one after another, so that what the creeping locust left the swarming locust will take. Piece by piece, happiness will disappear.

Yet, it would be a mistake to think that God has abandoned Judah and Jerusalem. In the midst of all the pain and suffering, God is going to save and restore. In fact, the nations who attack Jerusalem are being lured into a trap.

In that day, God will bring the nations to Jerusalem for battle. He will bring them to the valley of Jehoshaphat, which means "ADONAI judges."[8] The nations will think Israel to be easy prey. Judah and Jerusalem will fall at last. It's the same thing Egypt, Jordan, Syria, and other nations have thought in recent history.

Yet that valley will be a trap for the marauding armies of the nations. Those who sought to destroy Israel will be destroyed. The blood will run so deep, that God calls the valley a winepress running with the blood of his foes.[9]

But the blood will not taint the land forever. God will cleanse the land and restore it. The end result of Joel's drama is not a devastation of war, but rather a Judah and Jerusalem dripping sweet wine and dwelling securely forever.

ZECHARIAH'S WARRIOR GOD

Zechariah's warrior God story covers similar ground to Joel's. Zechariah lived in the time after many returned from Babylon. He did not know when God's plan to restore Israel would come. It seemed like it could come any time. The descendant of David, Zerubbabel, could take his throne and Israel could be a kingdom once again. His prophecies must have seemed all the more urgent considering the fact that they could come to pass at any time.

His drama of the warrior God begins with Judah and Jerusalem reeling from an attack.[10] The outlook seems hopeless until God pours out a spirit of favor on Judah and Jerusalem. This outpouring of favor or grace starts with the tents of David. Then something mysterious happens. The tribes all mourn a Pierced One.[11] They mourn for him as for an only son. This prophecy had to puzzle those who first heard it. It makes a great deal more sense now, now that we know who the Pierced One is.

After seeing the Pierced One, the tribes together call on Adonai and he descends in person to the Mount of Olives overlooking Jerusalem. He will personally destroy the armies attacking Jerusalem. He will create a valley through which they can escape as he, the warrior God, slaughters the armies of the nations.[12] He will cause the survivors of the nations to come to Jerusalem annually to worship Adonai.[13] He will cause his name to be One and make all the land of Israel as holy as the Holy of Holies in the Temple.[14]

YESHUA'S FIG TREE

Yeshua's fig tree is a much more limited tale. It is a vision of the end of the age, but it does not tell the full story. Rather, when asked about the timing of the end, Yeshua tells a story about delay and what to do while waiting.

The disciples pose a three-part question to Yeshua. Yeshua's complex answer comes in three parts corresponding to the three questions. And so, in the history of interpretation, Yeshua's discourse on the end times has been misunderstood. Many have failed to recognize the three parts.[15] The disciples asked when the Temple would be destroyed, when Yeshua would return, and what would be the sign of the end.[16] Yeshua answers the questions successively, and it is only in verse 32 that he addresses the timing of the end.

He says the end of the age will be abrupt. Yet, before that, there will be an age of delay, when terrible wars and persecutions will come. These are not the end, but they look like the end. Just as you see a fig tree budding and know summer is near, so the increase of wars and persecutions is a sign of the approaching climax of history.

Yet the age of delay should not throw people off. Just because God's foretelling is a long time in coming doesn't mean it won't happen. In fact, when it comes, the end will catch people unprepared. It will be as sudden as in the days of Noah. Two people will be next to each other and one will be taken in judgment and the other left alive. There won't be time to think. There won't be time to prepare.

Therefore, the subjects of the King are to be ready at all times. The end will come like a thief. The signs of the end are deceptive and repetitive, so that the end can come in any age.

Yeshua's story has elements of repeated history in it. Temple destructions and desecrations have happened repeatedly in Israel and at the end they will happen again. The Temple would be destroyed while the disciples were still alive, but that is not yet the end. Therefore, we are to watch Jerusalem as a farmer watches his fig tree.

JOHN'S SCROLL OF JUDGMENTS

Our last dramatic scene is from Revelation, also called the Apocalypse. Its author is John. The debates about which John are endless, but I am persuaded this is John who walked with Yeshua. John's message in the gospel is mostly about faith and love. In Revelation, the apostle of love delivers a message with teeth, even a message of horror.

John sees things that are symbolic. Interpretations vary, but the assumption here is that these are visions of events to come. John sees a scroll that is sealed, perhaps with wax or clay, at seven stopping points, seven places, as it is unrolled. The story of the seals of judgments agrees with the previous dramatic plots. Yet John adds dimensions not focused on before.

John is in Asia Minor. His congregations are mostly non-Jewish, which may be why he places more emphasis on the multitude from the nations. He fills in some gaps in the drama of the coming ages, placing non-Jews more fully into the story.

The same elements are there: the rise of a powerful king who opposes the true King, wars and plagues that wreak havoc not only in Israel but in the nations, and a great multitude from every tribe and tongue and nation who are dressed in white robes, saved by the Savior of Israel. If you read Revelation, you see in many places how John adds the faithful of the nations to the story without changing the plot.

THE COMMON THREADS OF ALL THE DRAMAS

What do the plots have in common? The King is coming to give a kingdom to his Holy Ones, essentially viewed as Israel and expanded in later understanding to include a great multitude from the nations. The establishment of this kingdom will come with great pain and war, but the ones who persevere to the end will be saved. The timing of the end is in the hands of the King and not the subjects. Our part is faith.

All these plots point to the coming of Messiah. The Days of Messiah must come before the final age, the World to Come. The Days of Messiah are the greatest days in human history. They are a necessary transition before human history will pass into a new age. After the Days of Messiah, it will no longer be the time of man's empires, but the dawning of the age of God and his people, together forever without any interruption or blemish.

CHAPTER 10

The Days of Messiah

I n his book *Everyman's Talmud*, Abraham Cohen explains the Jewish longing for Messiah. He quotes extensively from rabbinic literature, mostly literature from about 500 years after the time of Yeshua. At the very beginning of his chapter on the Messiah, Cohen makes a remarkable point:

> Whereas other peoples of antiquity placed their Golden Age in the dim and remote past, the Jews relegated it to the future. The prophets repeatedly allude to "the latter days," still unborn, as the period when the national greatness will reach its zenith.[1]

Unlike the Golden Age of Greece or the *Pax Romana* of Rome, Israel's time of greatness would be in the future. It is still future to us.

It is important to note that the vast majority of Christian thinkers and writers have denied that this time of Israel's greatness would ever come. Supersessionism, also called replacement theology, has been the norm in Christian understanding. Since the end of the Holocaust, there has been much improvement and many hopeful signs. But the Days of Messiah are coming to Israel with or without the faith of many in Christendom. At the center of Israel's future Golden Age is a single figure, the Son of David, the Anointed One, the Messiah. Messiah comes from a root word meaning anoint or to pour fragrant oil on someone. This was a ceremony for inaugurating kings and priests in the Ancient Near East and in Israel. The Messiah is the King, the one anointed to lead Israel in the Age to Come.

The speculation of the rabbis about the coming of Messiah is fascinating to read. Cohen says one rabbi from the 4th century actually denied that any Messiah would come. He believed that King Hezekiah had fulfilled all the prophecies.[2] Yet majority opinion was and is that Messiah has yet to be revealed. One glorious passage in the Talmud says that seven things pre-existed the world: Torah, repentance, Paradise, Hell, God's throne, the Temple, and the name of Messiah.[3]

In their scriptural discussions and debates, the rabbis colorfully played with possible names for Messiah. Some said he would be named after their teacher and found creative scriptural proofs. Others suggested names like *Tzemach*, the Branch, based on Zechariah 6:12, or Son of the Fallen, based on Amos 9:11.[4]

Interestingly, there is a tradition that the Days of Messiah will be preceded by a time of birth-pains, or the travail of Messiah. The rabbis said:

In the generation in which the son of David will come youths will insult their elders, the old will have to stand up before the young, daughter will revolt against her mother . . . and a son will feel no shame in the presence of his father. . . . Meeting places for study will be turned into brothels, the learning of the scribes will decay and sin-fearing men will be condemned.[5]

One very interesting tradition even says that the period of birth-pains will last seven years. The first year will be rain, then a year of famine, then starvation, then a year of plenty followed by more famine, the fifth year will be good, and in the sixth there will be voices from heaven. In the seventh there will be wars and then Messiah will come.[6] The biblical picture of a seven-year time of tribulation and of Armageddon is clear in this tradition.

How can we bring the Days of Messiah nearer? The rabbis also wrote about this question. In one place the Talmud says that repentance is great because it makes the time of redemption come sooner.[7] A well-known dictum is that, "If all Israel were to keep two Sabbaths according to the law, they would be redeemed forthwith."[8] The idea that we can bring the Days of Messiah sooner is hinted at in the New Testament, where Peter says, "as you wait for the Day of God and work to hasten its coming."[9]

Messiah is the king who comes from the line of David and brings about the restoration of Israel. He is also, according to Isaiah, a light to the nations, to the Gentiles. It might be helpful to list the prophecies about Messiah from the Hebrew scriptures:

General Messianic Prophecies

- Genesis 22:18 (Abraham's seed).
- Genesis 49:10 (Judah's scepter).
- Numbers 24:17–19 (The Star of Jacob).
- 2 Samuel 7:12–18 (The Son of God).
- Psalm 2 (The Anointed Son).
- Psalm 89 (The Davidic King).
- Psalm 110 (The Priest like Melchizedek).
- Amos 9:11 (The Fallen Booth of David).
- Micah 2:12–13 (The King who Breaks).

Prophecies of King Messiah

- Hosea 3:5 (David, their King).
- Micah 5:1-4 (A Ruler from of Old).
- Isaiah 9:1-7 (Light of Galilee, Prince of Peace).
- Isaiah 11:1-16 (Root of Jesse, Righteous Judge).
- Isaiah 61:1-3 (Healer of the Broken-Hearted).
- Jeremiah 23:5-6 (Branch of David).
- Jeremiah 30:21 (The Leader in the Last Days).
- Jeremiah 33:14-26 (Branch of David).
- Ezekiel 21:25-27 (The One to whom it Belongs).
- Ezekiel 34:23-21 (The One Shepherd).
- Ezekiel 37:24-28 (David, my Servant).
- Daniel 7:13-14 (Son of Man).
- Zechariah 9:9-10 (The King on a Donkey).

Prophecies of a Suffering Messiah

- Isaiah 42:1-4 (The Gentle Servant).
- Isaiah 49:1-7 (The Servant's Despair).
- Isaiah 52:13—53:12 (The Suffering Servant).
- Daniel 9:25-26 (The Anointed One Cut Off).
- Zechariah 12:10 (The Pierced One).

WHAT WILL THE DAYS OF MESSIAH BE LIKE?

The Days of Messiah are not the final days. There is yet an age to come after them. This is the opinion of part of the Christian world as well as the view of the Talmudic rabbis.[10] The rabbis of Israel thought of the Days of Messiah as an agricultural paradise. They spoke of grapes so large, a man would keep just one in his house and draw thirty measures of wine from it.[11] They spoke of grain and fruit growing much more rapidly than in this age. They even spoke of women bearing children daily![12]

In a rabbinic commentary on Exodus, the rabbis put their biblical genius to work figuring out ten things that will change in the Days of Messiah:

1. God will replace the sun as the light of this world (Isa. 60:19).
2. Healing waters will flow out from the Temple in Jerusalem (Ezek. 47:9).
3. Fruit will grow every month (Ezek. 47:12).
4. Ruined cities will all be rebuilt and there will be no waste places (Ezek. 16:55).
5. Jerusalem will be rebuilt with sapphires (Isa. 54:11).
6. Nature will be at peace with no more killing (Isa. 11:7).
7. Israel will have a covenant with the wild beasts (Hos. 2:18).
8. There will be no weeping in the world (Isa. 65:19).
9. Death will cease (Isa. 25:8).
10. There will be joy without groaning (Isa. 35:10).[13]

We can see how much the coming of Messiah sparked the imagination of the rabbis as they looked longingly on those days.

No wonder that Paul (remember, he is a Jew, of the Pharisaic party) described the coming of Yeshua back to this earth as "the blessed hope," which we eagerly wait for. What greater hope is there for mankind than the return of the King? The Days of Messiah are what we pray for when we say, as Yeshua taught us, "Your kingdom come, your will be done." Messiah is the hope and crown of Israel, the light and banner of the nations, the resurrector of the dead, the judge of all the earth, and the righteousness of Jerusalem.

THE HOPE AND CROWN OF ISRAEL

Every morning, afternoon, and evening, we pray in Judaism eighteen benedictions to God. One of the benedictions asks that the throne of David be established soon in Jerusalem. Another asks that the offspring of David will soon flourish in this world. These are prayers for the coming of Messiah. In words more pregnant with meaning than the editors of the prayer book probably realized, I find this footnote: "Here we are taught that the ultimate salvation of the Jewish people is possible only through the Davidic Messiah."[14]

The Jewish ache for Messiah to come is famously illustrated in the movie, *Fiddler on the Roof.* After a terrible pogrom, when the Russians would loot, pillage, and rape Jews, one of the men of the town says, "Rabbi, wouldn't now be a good time for Messiah to come?" Everyone sadly affirms that it would indeed.

There have been a number of mass movements of Jews following false Messiahs. The most famous was Shabbetai Tzvi in the 17th century. A large part of world Jewry got behind this movement. The Jewish people had been suffering and people put their hope in Messiah.

So it will be at the end of this age, when Israel is under attack from a multi-national army. The famous battle of Armageddon will be terrible. But at the end of that battle will be Messiah, standing with his feet on the Mount of Olives, rescuing the people of Jerusalem and slaying the armies who defied God's people.[15]

The prophecies about the Son of David who will come to rule this world are full of good news for Israel and Judah. Hosea says that one day Israel will seek after God and "David their king," and the latter days of Israel will be with God and his goodness.[16] Micah says the king whose origins are from days of old and who was born in Bethlehem will shepherd Israel as his flock.[17] Messiah will be a newly grown shoot from the cut off stump of Jesse, meaning the long deceased line of Davidic kings will be restored in Messiah.[18] He will give to the ones who mourn in Jerusalem a garland to replace their ashes.[19] He will restore the voice of the bridegroom and the bride in war-torn Jerusalem.[20]

So Yeshua, when he was here the first time, insisted that his work was for the Jewish people.[21] He came to end Israel's exile, if they would follow the way he was pointing. If not, he would leave until the day Israel would receive him. So Yeshua saw his mission as a mission to Israel and Jerusalem. Weeping over the city that rejected him, he said he would not return until the people of Jerusalem called for him as their bridegroom.[22]

THE LIGHT AND BANNER OF THE NATIONS

Yet Messiah did not come only for Israel and Judah. The promise to Abraham had said from the beginning that all the families of the earth would be blessed through Israel.[23] In Moses' last speech before he died, he told the children of Israel that God would one day make them jealous through those who are not a people.[24] The psalmist sang of the day when all the nations would worship before Adonai.[25]

Imagine what it must have been like for first century Jews. They were used to a minority of Romans who sympathized with Judaism. In their synagogues there were a number of Romans and Greeks who converted and joined the synagogue. There were also God-fearers, who often practiced the law and attended synagogue, but who did not convert.

But nothing could prepare them for the spreading Yeshua movement. Imagine a first century Jewish family living in a comfortable Roman insula in the suburbs. One day their Roman neighbor is acting like a Roman, pouring out the first sip of each glass of wine as an offering to household gods. The next day he is talking about Messiah.

What is this Gentile doing talking about Messiah? Isn't he our Messiah? Do the Romans have to take that away from us too?

In one of Isaiah's Servant Songs, God is speaking to the Servant, the Messiah. God says it is not enough for the Servant to restore the tribes of Israel. God has bigger plans for the Servant. He will also be a light to the nations, to the Gentiles, and God's salvation will extend to the very ends of the earth.[26]

He is Israel's Messiah and the Messiah of the Gentiles as well. In the last days, the Gentiles will flock to Jerusalem to see Messiah and hear his teaching. They will come to a restored and greatly enlarged Jerusalem. They will come to the house of God, the Temple, in Jerusalem, which will be the throne of Messiah.[27]

THE RESURRECTOR OF THE DEAD

Of all the peoples on the earth, only the Jewish people incorporated bodily resurrection in their religion. The first hint of it, perhaps, is in Isaiah 26:19, where he speaks of the dead returning to life, awaking, and singing for joy. The teaching is more clearly spelled out in Daniel 12:2, where those who sleep awake either to everlasting life or everlasting punishment.

In the eighteen benedictions of Judaism, we pray, "You are eternally mighty, my Lord, resuscitator of the dead are you; abundantly able to save."[28] The footnote in *The Artscroll Siddur* says, " . . . . the literal resuscitation of the dead, which will take place in the Messianic Age."[29]

Messiah himself said, "The time is coming when all who are in the grave will hear his voice and come out—those who have done good to a resurrection of life, and those who have done evil to a resurrection of judgment."[30] It's true. Messiah is the one who will call us from our graves, or, if we are still alive, will change us in an instant.

Paul says Messiah will descend with a shout and a great trumpet blast. The faithful dead will rise first and join Messiah. The faithful who are alive will ascend with them into the clouds to be with Messiah in the air. From that time we will never be separated from Messiah again.[31] In another place he says this will all happen suddenly, in the blink of an eye, at the final trumpet.[32]

I Corinthians 15 is a long and in-depth exploration of the topic of resurrection. Among other things, Paul says that our new bodies will be continuous and discontinuous with our present ones. People frequently wonder what age we will be, if we will be a perfect weight, if we will be more beautiful. Paul says mysteriously that when you sow a seed, it dies first, and then becomes something much greater than the seed.[33] He says the difference in beauty between our present bodies and our eternal ones is like comparing earthly bodies to the sun, moon, and stars![34] Our eternal bodies will be undying and perfectly whole and more glorious than any body we have ever seen on earth.

But most of all, we will be with Messiah in those days and forever. He will resurrect us and keep us with him forever.

But not all who enter the Days of Messiah will be resurrected. There will be on the earth, at the time of Yeshua's coming, a large population of people who survived the wars and plagues of Revelation. Many of them will not be followers of Yeshua when he comes. They will not be changed, as we are. They will enter the Days of Messiah unchanged.

And so you have the odd thing about the Days of Messiah. There will be immortals and mortals dwelling together on the earth. And the Judge over all will be Messiah Yeshua.

THE JUDGE OF ALL THE EARTH

When Messiah comes, "he will not judge by what his eyes see or decide by what his ears hear, but he will judge the impoverished justly; he will decide fairly for the humble of the land."[35] Anyone who has run afoul of our modern systems of justice knows how human justice is flawed. We also know that not all injustices are righted and many suffer under the wrongs of oppression, hurts, insults, slander, and false accusation.

This world cries out for justice. The blood of the slain speaks to God and he hears. We have not been our brother's keeper, as Cain sarcastically commented to God. Many people have felt along with the psalmist, "How long, ADONAI? How long must my enemy dominate me?"[36] The lament of the Teacher in Ecclesiastes calls out for a true Judge: "I saw the tears of the oppressed and they had no one to comfort them."[37] Job's question deserves an answer: "Why do the wicked go on living, grow old and keep increasing their power?"[38]

You can see it when you watch the news or read what is happening in our world. Justice is perverted. The wrong people, inevitably, are in charge. The right people, once they are in charge, tend to turn into the wrong kind of people. Where is there a good king who will make the land whole again? Where is justice?

Messiah will bring that justice. He will judge with righteousness. He is the Judge of all the earth.

We can imagine how it will be when the Judge, our Messiah, comes. The wicked armies of the world will be slain at the very outset of his kingdom. He will send out the faithful, the resurrected believers from all time, into the earth to reign with him.[39] In his name the faithful will restore peace, justice, and harmony to the world. The King will begin redeeming and repairing the hurts of millennia of crime, oppression, abuse, slavery, slander, and terror. Swords will be beaten into plowshares, as growing fantastic crops will replace violence as the pastime of the world.[40]

THE RIGHTEOUSNESS OF JERUSALEM

There is a beautiful promise in Jeremiah 23:6:"In his days Judah will be saved and Israel will dwell securely.And this is the name by which he will be called: 'The Lord is our righteousness.'" Jerusalem, the city, which often has rebelled against Adonai, will someday accept that righteousness comes only from him. God alone can make us righteous.

Isaiah wrote of a day when the Torah would go out from Zion to all the earth. In the synagogue today, as we open the Ark, the piece of furniture that houses a handwritten scroll of the Torah, we conclude our prayer by saying, "For out of Zion will go forth the Torah and the word of the Lord from Jerusalem." We are quoting Isaiah 2:3 as we chant these words in the beautiful synagogue liturgy.

What does it mean that Adonai will be the righteousness of Jerusalem? What does it mean that God's Torah will go out from Zion in the Days of Messiah?

There is a curious fact about the Temple in those days.There will be no Ark of the Covenant in the Holy of Holies.[41] Rather, all the nations will be gathered to Jerusalem and they will call Jerusalem the Throne of Adonai.[42] That is, in place of the Ark, the throne of Adonai will be there. How will it be there?

It will be there because Messiah will take his throne in the Temple. Perhaps this is partially what Paul had in mind when he said of Messiah that God has made him our wisdom and our righteousness.[43] Messiah will be in Jerusalem, on his throne, sending out justice and Torah to the earth. Under his kingship, Adonai will be our righteousness. Thus, in a sense, Messiah is the righteousness of Jerusalem.

LONGING FOR MESSIAH

Wouldn't this be a good time for Messiah? History has shown that people long for Messiah to come especially in times of suffering. But wouldn't any time be a good time for Messiah to come?

He will bring joy we have never experienced before. He will bring transformation when we meet him in the air. He will bring an end to death and suffering. He will bring justice in a world filled with oppression and slander. He will bring real peace, the kind that lasts and exists not only between nations but also between father and mother and daughter and son. He will bring singing and dancing and laughter to Jerusalem again. He will bring joy beyond weeping.

How many of us pray as Yeshua taught us, "Your kingdom come, your will be done"? How many of us expect that we can, as Peter suggested, hasten the coming of Messiah?[44] How many of us pray, as the Jewish prayer book instructs, "May he give reign to his kingship in your lifetimes and in your days ... swiftly and soon"?[45]

Our longing should be like that expressed by Paul:

For God's grace, which brings deliverance, has appeared to all people. It teaches us to renounce godlessness and worldly pleasures, and to live self-controlled, upright and godly lives now, in this age; while continuing to expect the blessed fulfillment of our certain hope, which is the appearing of the Sh'khinah [glory] of our great God and the appearing of our Deliverer, Yeshua the Messiah.[46]

Shouldn't we be longing for Messiah at all times, good and bad? What better longing could there be?

CHAPTER 11

Love

Love, so cheaply used here in this present world, will be the greatest thing in the World to Come. "Love can tell, and love alone, whence the million stars were strewn,"[1] said poet Robert Bridges. Love is a great mystery to us. In love we find our greatest heartaches, the most disappointment, and yet the most potential of anything we experience in life. It can be so cheap, so common, so exploited for selfishness, and yet we are drawn to its potential for selflessness. It is true what the poet Samuel Daniel said, "Love is a sickness full of woes, all remedies refusing."[2]

"Give all to love; obey thy heart,"[3] said Emerson. And sometimes we get a glimmer of that kind of total commitment, faithfulness, and willing submission. "I want to die while you love me, and never, never see the glory of this perfect day grow dim or cease to be!"[4] said Georgia Douglas Johnson. Romantic love often motivates declarations of total commitment that rarely endure. Yet we celebrate the thought even if we find it rarely fulfilled.

William Blake, perhaps, said it best:

> Love seeketh not itself to please,
> Nor for itself hath any care.
> But for another gives its ease,
> And builds a Heaven in Hell's despair.[5]

Yet, even he was skeptical and he wrote another quatrain, in which a skeptic decries the reality of love as it is commonly practiced:

> Love seeketh only Self to please,
> To bind another to Its delight:
> Joys in another's loss of ease,
> And builds a Hell in Heaven's despite.

Love can be in the service of God or it can become a terrible god of its own.

Still, love is worth celebrating. For all the pains it causes in its imperfect forms, we sense in love something so grand, something so transcendent, it truly is the closest glimpse of heaven on earth.

Love comes in many forms. The sharp ache of romantic love, or *eros*, is most celebrated in poetry, movie, and fiction. To one degree or another, few human beings have failed to experience this love, if only for a fleeting moment. The warm comfort of affection, often associated with family, is a kind of love we hope to find if we don't do something to ruin its possibility. The bright laughter of friendship is an under-appreciated love and once inspired David to say he had loved a friend more deeply than any woman.[6]

Then there is plain love, *agape*, as the ancients called it. It is a word that covers all the kinds of love. It is behind every love and yet it is unique and can be singled out. It is the motive to seek another's good rather than your own. It is present in romance, affection, and friendship. Yet it can exist even for a stranger. It is, plainly, just love.

GOD AND LOVE

Love is the greatest fly in the materialist ointment. Those who believe human origins are random, merely a gathering of molecules evolving from simple organisms to the mighty and complex human person we are today, cannot really explain love.

Supposedly our great aspirations to other human beings are mere hormones and related to impulses to mate and to survive at peace with neighbors. It's not just that we rebel at such a cheapening of love, a thing we feel to be much greater than chemical and electrical reactions in our synapses. It is that purely material origins cannot explain the experience of love.

Love is a glimpse of heaven. God is love, said John.[7] If we open our eyes to truly see, we can readily believe it.

The things that love makes men and women do are beautiful, even when they are flawed. A mother gets up early and goes to bed late, working without any expectation of reward for love of her family. A man would give his life in an instant to save his child or his wife and maybe even a stranger. The Bible's ode to love says it well, "If a man offered for love all the wealth of his house, it would be utterly scorned."[8] There is nothing we value more than love, even in the form of cheap substitutes and all the more for the real thing.

Evolution as a theory of origins is mostly a theory of self-preservation and promotion. A limited amount of social exchange or familial sacrifice is perhaps understandable. Evolution could explain sacrifices made for the greater good of the tribe, perhaps. Yet we know love to be so much more.

Furthermore, love is peculiarly human. We see lesser forms in the animal world, but there is something in human love that far exceeds animal lust and even animal affection. You have only to look at the mating rituals of most animals to see the brute instinct to produce offspring brooks no tenderness in the act of reproduction. As Rob Bell noted when he and his family observed lions mating, "They aren't lying out there in that field thinking, 'I just really want to know that you love me for more than my body.'"[9]

The motive of love rises far above self-preservation and any form of survival of the fittest. For courtly romance, many knights and lords threw away their lives for a love they would never consummate. For pure *agape*, an adult will risk or even give their life to save an unknown child in danger. For friendship, a kind of love that has little evolutionary motive, a man or woman will risk all that is dear to them.

God is love. In love we see God. Love needs some better explanation than hormones and tribal preservation instincts. Love is a glimpse of the World to Come.

LOVE NEVER ENDS

1 Corinthians 13 is perplexing. Paul is not known for his poetic grace. He is much loved for his theological depth, but even among the apostles he had a reputation as a difficult though profound writer.[10] Yet of all the literature of the world, 1 Corinthians 13 stands out as belonging with the finest. As a purely literary composition it rivals the best poems and the greatest philosophical works and ethical treatises. 1 Corinthians 13 would be a classic even if it weren't in the Bible.

What moved Paul to write such a beautiful work? He had a rare understanding of heaven. He once was taken there, either literally or in a vision, and saw inexpressible things.[11] I Corinthians 13 is the kind of writing we might expect from such a man, shown more than most men about the life to come.

He begins with a principle that cuts to the heart of any man-made system of living. The issue he dealt with specifically here might seem strange to most modern people. Paul needed to persuade some religious people that miraculous powers could not hold a candle to love. But the formula works for any system of power and status. Wealth, power, and fame, to any degree, cannot hold a candle to love.

Not even religious sacrifice can compare to love. Paul says it is possible to give all to the poor and to do so out of other motives than love. Love is better than sacrifice, and sacrifice for anyone is only meaningful if done for love.

Paul's definition of love is that elusive thing we are trying to grasp but cannot completely achieve. In all the failed relationships, cheap encounters with sex, miserable fights with a spouse, failed promises of continuing friendship, and so on, we were seeking this very thing. In a phrase, love is selfless-giving. It is patient, kind, ready to submit for love's sake, and purely selfless. Love is forgiving and seeks the good of the other even when the other is undeserving.

Love never ends. That statement is literally true. All the laughable promises of undying love that never even came close to fulfillment cannot erase the truth. Love never ends.

The things that the Corinthians boasted about would all end. The ability to prophesy is great, but what will anyone need to prophesy about in the World to Come? It will all be here. This is true of other status symbols as well. Lovers of money would do well to heed the joke about the man who tried to bribe Peter to get into heaven. He brought a bag of gold. Peter took one look and said, "Why would I need paving stones?"

Love never ends. The greatest virtues of God's people are faith, hope, and love. Yet a day is coming, Paul says, when we will not need faith or hope. Who will need faith when God is immediately present and not hidden from us? Who will need hope when all that we hoped for is there, in the World to Come?

But we will need and enjoy love. Love never ends.

MAKE THE MOST OF LOVE

Beauty and desire are good things. They foreshadow heaven. But love is greater even than these. You can experience a foretaste of heaven by taking in a beautiful scene or imagining desires finding eternal fulfillment. Yet the most accurate foretaste of the World to Come is between the self and the other, between the lover and the beloved, between friend and friend, father and mother and child—even between you and the stranger if you love with perfect love.

Nothing brings us so high, so close to the tops of the mountains of God, as love. Every selfless act, from the smallest hug to the greatest sacrifice, is eternal. The deeds of the righteous live on forever into glory.

In two places, Paul advises us to make the most of the time, by doing good deeds and particularly toward those outside our communities.[12] If love never ends and if God is love, then we have too little time to give all the love we should. A chance to show love today may be gone tomorrow. Love given too late is as bad as no love at all.

The World to Come is the place where all the deeds of love will live on and where love rules the very order of existence. The World to Come is not another world, but this world made better. The New Jerusalem is coming down. The New Earth is this Earth remade. Who knows but some act of love we give to family, friends, or, more likely, to a stranger, might not be a brick in the wall of the New Jerusalem. God is redeeming and perfecting this world. It would be foolish to think he won't use us.

CHAPTER 12

The Holy One

When we enter the World to Come, Revelation 22:4 says we will see the face of the Holy One. I John 3:2 says that we will see him as he is and we will be like him. To see the face of the Holy One is the greatest thing in the World to Come.

Yet, deep down, if we really admit it, many of us are concerned that God will be boring. To see him might be an awesome spectacle at first, but like the fading thrill of seeing Niagara Falls or the Grand Canyon, we worry that the World to Come will be a fading thrill.

Some people's vision of the World to Come is a prolonged worship service. Maybe we imagine a place that is very white and very bright. In front if us somewhere we may picture a throne with a brightness on it that exceeds any star. Perhaps we can for a moment, in such a vision, capture a bit of a thrill.

But we've all been in worship services. If the music goes on for half an hour, we can perhaps maintain a sense of awe. But when people stand for worship, there comes a time when they want to sit down. Worship can be tiring. It can become boring.

Perhaps the worship service there will be better, we tell ourselves. Maybe we will enjoy it longer. How long? Will we stand for a day? A year? A century? Will a place of bright light, pure whiteness, and prolonged worship with people and angels be an eternal thrill?

Not only is this vision of the World to Come completely wrong. This vision of God is also wrong.

Randy Alcorn, in his book *Heaven*, put is this way:

All secondary joys are *derivative* in nature. They cannot be separated from God. Flowers are beautiful for one reason—God is beautiful. Rainbows are stunning because God is stunning.

> Puppies are delightful because God is delightful. Sports are fun
> because God is fun. Study is rewarding because God is reward-
> ing. Work is fulfilling because God is fulfilling.[1]

Alcorn's point is philosophically profound. We believe that God is
the author of all reality. In this reality, we experience various joys and
believe they have their source in God. We suspect that of all things in
our experience, the joys are the ones that will remain in the coming
world. We trust that this is what God is doing as he prepares a New
Earth for us.

Therefore, every joy we experience has its counterpart in God
and the perfect joy that will be in him. Alcorn says of those who
disregard earthly pleasures and look only for some sort of spiritual
pleasure, "Ironically, some people who are most determined to avoid
the sacrilege of putting things before God miss a thousand daily opportunities to thank him, praise him, and draw near to him, because
they imagine they shouldn't enjoy the very things he made to help us
know him and love him."[2]

BLESSINGS, GOD, AND THE WORLD TO COME

In Judaism, the joys of the World to Come are not separated from
the earthly joys that point to them. Rather, every joy (and hardship)
encountered here and now is an occasion for a blessing.

One of the blessings recited at a Jewish wedding says, "Blessed
are you, O Lord our God, King of the Universe, who created joy
and gladness." How often do we fail to recite such a blessing to
God? More importantly, how often do we miss the chance of seeing
that earthly joys are derived from him? The joy of the bride and the
bridegroom is perhaps the closest picture on earth to the joy of being in God's presence.

Do you think a lucky groom is bored on his wedding day or
that a fortunate bride would rather be somewhere else? Neither
will there be any sense of boredom in the World to Come. The
Bible again and again uses the image of a bride and bridegroom to
describe God's relationship to Israel and the church.

Not least of the joys on a wedding day is the promise of sexual intimacy that it holds for the couple being married. Rob Bell explores the reason sexuality is used as an image of heavenly bliss:

We read that in this city "nothing impure will ever enter into it." Isn't that what sex is supposed to be for people in its greatest moment? When it is free from power and coercion and manipulation and agendas and fears, when it is simply two people giving all of themselves to each other, holding nothing back?. . . For many people sex is brief moments when everything is okay with the world, even if it isn't. It's escape from the pain and suffering and brokenness of life.... In Revelation, God announces, "I am making everything new." Isn't that the longing of every embrace, of every act of love, of sex itself? To start again, to give yourself away, again, to try again for hope and healing and restoration?[3]

God boring? Hardly. He's no more boring than the first real act of love we ever experienced. He is the bridegroom.

It's quite likely that sex itself will not exist in the World to Come. Sex is derivative. It derives from God who made it. It is a sign in this life of the reality of who God is. That complete giving, total openness to another, is likely a picture of the union with God that the faithful have to look forward to. We do not, as some mystics erroneously proposed, lose ourselves in God. We remain us and he remains himself. But our union is something more joyful and profound, like the joy of perfect, loving sex.

There are many other derivative joys in life. In Judaism there are blessings for occasions when we encounter such joys. Hearing thunder or seeing lightning is a moment when we understand how much bigger the universe is than we had imagined. So we say a blessing, "Blessed are you, O Lord our God, King of the Universe, who makes the work of creation. Blessed are you, O Lord our God, King of the Universe, for his strength and his power fill the universe."

Judaism teaches an enjoyment of this world in God and not apart from God. This way of looking at life puts back together things that should never have been separated: the physical and the spiritual.

It was the Greeks who, following Plato, imagined that the physical is temporary and inferior. It is asceticism, not biblical religion, that forbids sex, food, drink, and pleasure.

Judaism sees many occasions to find a picture of God in the derived joys of life. Upon seeing fruit trees in the spring, we are to say, "Blessed are you, O Lord our God, King of the Universe, for nothing is lacking in his universe, and he created in it good creatures and good trees, to cause humankind pleasure with them." Upon seeing a beautiful person, tree, or landscape, we bless him for "putting such things in his universe."

When we enter the World to Come, we will see the face of the Holy One. But we forget that right now we see him too. Paul said, "For ever since the creation of the universe his invisible qualities - both his eternal power and his divine nature - have been clearly seen, because they can be understood from what he has made."[4]

THE EVERLASTING UNION

In the Talmud, there is a story that illustrates the majesty and splendor of the Holy One:

A Caesar said to R. Joshua ben Hananiah, "I want to see your God." R. Joshua: "You cannot see him." Caesar: "Nevertheless, I want to see him." So R. Joshua had Caesar stand facing the sun during the summer solstice of Tammuz and said to him, "Look directly at the sun." Caesar: "I cannot." R. Joshua: "If you say of the sun, which is only one of the servitors standing before the Holy One, blessed be He, 'I cannot look directly at it,' how much less could you look at the Presence [Shekhinah} itself."[5]

We have no need to fear that God might turn out to be boring. Not only is it a false image to imagine that the World to Come will be an eternal worship service involving singing and praying through the eons. It is also a false image to imagine God in any limited form.

God is not a bright light on a throne. He is certainly not a kind-ly, bearded old man in a white robe. He is wiser than all wisdom accumulated by humankind through the ages. He is more innately good than any expression of selfless love we have ever experienced. He is mightier than the vast nebulae and more enduring than any ocean or range of mountains. His depths are beyond plumbing out.

Christian thinkers have also sought to understand the depths of God. Augustine said:

God himself, who is the Author of virtue, shall be our reward. As there is nothing better or greater than God himself, God has promised us himself. God shall be the end of all our desires, who will be seen without end, loved without cloy, and praised without weariness.[6]

The key phrase here is "end of all our desires." It does not mean that our desires will cease. The word end has two meanings: termination and goal. God is not the termination of all our desires, but the goal of them. Every earthly desire points to a corresponding reality in God. And we will love him and be loved by him without any hint of cloying sweetness that becomes too much. There will be no weariness in our enjoyment of God.

Jonathan Edwards put it a different way:

God is the highest good of the reasonable creature, and the enjoyment of him is the only happiness with which our souls can be satisfied. To go to heaven fully to enjoy God, is infinitely better than the most pleasant accommodations here. Fathers and mothers, husbands, wives, children, or the company of earthly friends, are but shadows. But the enjoyment of God is the substance. These are but scattered beams, but God is the sun. These are but streams, but God is the fountain. These are but drops, but God is the ocean.[7]

All of this puts a new spin on the idea of seeing God face to face. The problem is that we cannot truly imagine what that will be like. Our religious communities have sometimes created inadequate pictures for us of the unending delight we will have in God and he in us.

The World to Come is a place of unadulterated joy, adventure, desire, and satisfaction. We've never experienced that, since all earthly satisfactions diminish with time.

Yet chief of all the joys will be God. Yeshua once assured his disciples shortly before his death that he was going away to prepare a place for them in the World to Come.[8] Later in his teaching he assured them of the true joy of this place he went to prepare. He said that his disciples would come to have the certainty that Yeshua was in the Father, they in Yeshua, and Yeshua in them.[9] That is to say, that the place Yeshua is preparing us in the World to Come is about being with God. At the end of his prayer over the disciples in John 17, Yeshua further clarified the great joy that awaited his disciples and all who would believe after them:

Father, I want those you have given me to be with me where I am; so that they may see my glory, which you have given me because you loved me before the creation of the world. Righteous Father, the world has not known you, but I have known you, and these people have known that you sent me. I made your name known to them, and I will continue to make it known; so that the love with which you have loved me may be in them, and I myself may be united with them.[10]

Yeshua, who alone of all people who have ever lived on this earth, knows the depths of heaven, says that the great joy of it all will be the glory of God. He longed for his disciples to see and understand a glory that transcends all mortal experience.

It is the glory of the being of God. The mountains in the World to Come will draw us ever deeper in, more and more to that glory that is greater than all joys and satisfactions.

CHAPTER 13

Further Up and Further In

In C. S. Lewis's *The Great Divorce*, the protagonist sees something strange and inviting when his bus arrives from hell for a vacation in heaven. Very far away into the west he see what might be a cloud-bank or possibly a mountain range. He says, "Sometimes I could make out in it steep forests, far-withdrawing valleys, and even mountain cities perched on inaccessible summits."[1]

At this point in his heavenly vacation, the protagonist has no idea what those western mountains represent. Later he finds out that the solid people, the citizens of that place, who have been coming to visit, have been coming out of those mountains. The character of George MacDonald, who is Lewis's solid person host, says to him, "Every one of us lives only to journey further and further into the mountains."[2]

Lewis's picture is of residents of the World to Come journeying always nearer and nearer to God, always progressing along the way to deeper knowledge of him. That picture evokes a question: Will we know God instantly upon entering the World to Come or will we always grow in the knowledge of him?

Paul says, "Now I know partly; then I will know fully, just as God has fully known me."[3] This might seem to cut off any speculation on our question of knowledge, God, and eternity. Read in one particular way, Paul could be read as indicating that we will know God completely as he completely knows us.

Yet there are reasons to doubt this reading. In the first place, it is an assumption and only an assumption if we imagine we will ever be omniscient. Only God is all-knowing in the present and we may fairly well assume in the future as well. There is no promise anywhere of omniscience. Yet to know God completely would mean to be omniscient, since God is infinite.

There is a better way to read Paul's saying. Knowing fully does not necessarily mean knowing completely. Paul is contrasting in I Corinthians 13 his distorted view of reality from the standpoint of mortal existence. That is, we have a limited perspective here. There are things too wonderful for us to comprehend. From our limited perspective, much that we perceive about God is mysterious and even erroneous. But then, when we enter the World to Come, we will not know in such a distorted way, but in a perfectly unrestrained way. There will be no barrier of understanding and we will see clearly.

It is not necessarily true that God will "upload" all insight about his attributes and nature into our brains the moment we arrive in paradise (or should I say the moment paradise arrives here).

It seems that this world is a shadow of the World to Come. In this world we have joy in learning and growing. It is reasonable to imagine that learning and growing will continue in the World to Come.

But someone will argue that infinity is, after all, a very long time. We will have infinite time to learn and surely that means we will be omniscient eventually.

Infinity is a difficult concept to grasp. My feeble mind can only respond that on the subject of God and the universe there is infinite material to learn and infinity is only barely enough time to do it. Besides, we may not even understand our relationship to time as it will be then. Perhaps Lewis's image of an unending range of mountains off into the west is reasonably accurate. Perhaps the World to Come will be about always going further up and further in, always further and further into the mountains.

FROM HERE TO ETERNITY

We're always thinking of the World to Come as a future place in a future age. We live in this present age and we await the age to come. We live on this earth and await the New Earth. We see a discontinuity.

Yet there is another perspective. The World to Come is present already in part. Eternal life has already begun. The future age has broken into the now. The World to Come is this world perfected and not a replacement world yet to be made.

There are a number of ways in which we can see that we are already journeying into those mountains. One of the simplest and most overlooked teachings of the Bible is that we can work now to lay up reward in the World to Come. Yeshua said:

> Do not store up for yourselves wealth here on earth, where moths and rust destroy, and burglars break in and steal. Instead, store up for yourselves wealth in heaven, where neither moth nor rust destroys, and burglars do not break in or steal.[4]

Suppose you were taking an extended trip to another country and you had a way to start depositing money for the trip in an account in that country. In some ways, part of you would already be in that country. There are things we can do here that will affect our lives in the World to Come. Our work in the present world should be active engagement in Tikkun Olam, leaving the world better than we found it. Love and selfless deeds will never disappear, but will have their reward in the hereafter. Some will only be there because of an act of love, one person to another. No selfless act will be forgotten.

No wonder Paul advises us, "Focus your minds on the things above, not on things here on earth."[5] The New Earth is the true country and this world is a place of sojourn, a temporary home. In a beautiful discourse, the writer of Hebrews describes the Patriarchs and faithful men and women from the Hebrew scriptures. They lived under the shadow of unfulfilled promises. Abraham was a resident alien in a land that was promised to one day belong to his family. Yet he had joy in the promise even though it had not been fulfilled. His mind never lost sight of the promise, but "he was looking forward to the city with permanent foundations, of which the architect and builder is God."[6]

The rabbis realized this very truth and they loved to speak of the World to Come. Some of the oldest sayings of the rabbis are recorded in the *Pirkei Avot* (Sayings of the Fathers), which is included in the Mishnah. In *Pirkei Avot 4:16* we read:

> R. Jacob said: This world is like unto a vestibule before the
> World to Come; prepare thyself in the vestibule, so that thou
> mayest enter the banqueting hall.[7]

Like Yeshua, who came before them, the rabbis recognized that this life matters in the life to come.

There are preparations to make for the World to Come, just as a trip to a foreign country. Yeshua spoke to Martha of Bethany, whose brother was lying dead in a tomb. He told her of the most important preparation for the World to Come: "I AM the Resurrection and the Life! Whoever puts his trust in me will live, even if he dies; and everyone living and trusting in me will never die."[8] In another place, Yeshua assured his disciples, "Whoever acknowledges me in the presence of others I will also acknowledge in the presence of my Father in heaven."[9]

Those preparing for the journey to the World to Come cannot wait until later to be prepared. Eternal life does not wait until death to begin. The coming age has broken into the present age. The time for Tikkun Olam is now. As the rabbis said, we are already in the vestibule, the foyer. If we want to enter God's banquet hall, we had better be ready. We had best come with faith in the King, Yeshua. And not only ready to merely enter, we ought to have wealth prepared for the World to Come, wealth that starts with love and selfless deeds done for others in this world.

THE HEAVENLY BODY

Some people like hiking and would enjoy trekking through forest paths and climbing over mountain passes. Some love the great outdoors and could relate to the joy of tending sheep under a blue sky on fertile, rolling hills. For others, the whole thing sounds tiring.

There are some parts of the World to Come that we prepare ourselves for and others which only God can prepare us for. The characters visiting heaven in Lewis's *The Great Divorce* found that they were not solid enough for that world, not substantial enough to even lift the petal of a daisy. For those faithful who will inhabit the World to Come, God has revealed to us a mystery. We will all be changed.

Paul gives an extended discourse on this is 1 Corinthians 15. He says at the final trumpet we will all be changed, "For this material which can decay must be clothed with imperishability, this which is mortal must be clothed with immortality."[10]

There are a number of images from this world which Paul can use as analogies to explain the changed body we will have then. One analogy is that of a seed. It falls to the ground and dies. Then the small kernel of wheat becomes something much greater, a stalk bearing many seeds.[11]

In a different analogy, Paul compares earthly bodies with heavenly ones:

Further, there are heavenly bodies and earthly bodies; but the beauty of heavenly bodies is one thing, while the beauty of earthly bodies is something else. The sun has one kind of beauty, the moon another, the stars yet another; indeed, each star has its own individual kind of beauty. So it is with the resurrection of the dead. When the body is "sown," it decays; when it is raised, it cannot decay. When sown, it is without dignity; when raised, it will be beautiful. When sown, it is weak; when raised, it will be strong. When sown, it is an ordinary human body; when raised, it will be a body controlled by the Spirit. If there is an ordinary human body, there is also a body controlled by the Spirit.[12]

People have many questions about their bodies in the World to Come. Will I be old or young? Will I be overweight or sculpted like an athlete or something else? Will I look at all the same?

The Bible affirms that you will always be you. Yet the mystery is that your heavenly body will be different, better. Looking at the stars, we can only imagine the glory we will have then. We will be fit to enter that New Earth and explore its mountains, forests, and fertile valleys.

GETTING A HEAD START

We can already imagine those mountains in the west. We can already taste the new wine and smell the green hills. The World to Come is like our heavenly body. It will be different and yet the same. The mortal, dying world will put on the immortality of the undying lands. Death will end. Life will reign forever.

So just as our present bodies are going to continue and yet be changed, so this world will continue but will be changed. Peter says, "That Day will bring on the destruction of the heavens by fire, and the elements will melt from the heat; but we, following along with his promise, wait for new heavens and a new earth, in which righteousness will be at home."[13] Likely the destruction Peter speaks of will not be a total destruction of earth, but a remaking and reshaping of its surface. The dead things and decaying things will be gone. Only life and goodness will be remade.

The reality of the New Earth led to a conclusion in Peter's message. Since the world is going to become so changed, so much better, how should we live? Said Peter, "You should lead holy and godly lives."[14] That is, in the present, we should live for the future.

C. S. Lewis put it well from the Christian point of view:

> If you read history, you will find that the Christians who did the most for the present world were just those who thought most of the next. The Apostles themselves, who set on foot the conversion of the Roman Empire, the great men who built up the Middle Ages, the English Evangelicals who abolished the Slave Trade, all left their mark on Earth, precisely because their minds were occupied with Heaven....Aim at Heaven and you will get earth "thrown in"; aim at earth and you will get neither.[15]

And so, though we don't completely understand it, there is such a thing as treasure in heaven, wealth in the World to Come. All of the faithful, the followers of Yeshua from Israel and the nations, we can get a head start into those mountains. The journey has already begun, for those with enough faith to believe in it.

The World to Come is present for us in two ways. First, we can enjoy it already. Since we know that every joy here is derived from God and is therefore eternal, we ought to enjoy this life with a view to the World to Come:

So look out a window. Take a walk. Talk with your friend. Use your God-given skills to paint or draw or build a shed or write a book. But imagine it—all of it—in its original condition. The happy dog with the wagging tail, not the snarling beast, beaten and starved. The flowers unwilted, the grass undying, the blue sky without pollution. People smiling and joyful, not angry, depressed, and empty. If you're not in a particularly beautiful place, close your eyes and envision the most beautiful place you've ever been—complete with palm trees, raging rivers, jagged mountains, waterfalls, and snow drifts.[16]

And in addition to enjoying the shadows of the World to Come in this world, we can also be present there in another way. Those who want to get further up and further in, to draw nearer and nearer to the unfathomable beauty of God, can already make some progress into those mountains.

The rabbis put it this way, "Better is one hour of repentance and good deeds in this world than the whole life of the World to Come; and better is one hour of blissfulness of spirit in the World to Come than the whole life of this world."[17] It is a paradox. Why is this saying true? It is because in this world we can right wrongs, show love to the hurting, and overcome sin. In the World to Come there will be no wrongs, no hurting, and no sin. So the time for good deeds is now. In that sense, one hour here can be better than the whole of eternity there. Yet one hour there is better than all the joys of this world put together.

So we have little time to waste. The World to Come is to be enjoyed now as we wait for it to come then. If we want to get further into those mountains, we'd best start living as citizens of a better country. We'd better follow the example of Abraham and others, who looked for a a city not built by human hands. The mountains are calling us further in.

APPENDIX A

Scripture Compendium

This compendium is not complete and does not attempt to be. Still, few realize how many passages in the Bible address the World to Come in one way or another. These verses are provided as a quick reference and are organized by topic. There are some repeats as many passages cover multiple themes related to the World to Come. I pray that the words God spoke through prophets and apostles will stir in you a desire to know the reality of which they speak.

The Regathering of Israel

DEUTERONOMY 30:1-6. When the time arrives that all these things have come upon you, both the blessing and the curse which I have presented to you; and you are there among the nations to which *ADONAI* your God has driven you; then, at last, you will start thinking about what has happened to you; and you will return to *ADONAI* your God and pay attention to what he has said, which will be exactly what I am ordering you to do today - you and your children, with all your heart and all your being. At that point, *ADONAI* your God will reverse your exile and show you mercy; he will return and gather you from all the peoples to which *ADONAI* your God scattered you. If one of yours was scattered to the far end of the sky, *ADONAI* your God will gather you even from there; he will go there and get you. *ADONAI* your God will bring you back into the land your ancestors possessed, and you will possess it; he will make you prosper there, and you will become even more numerous than your ancestors. Then *ADONAI* your God will circumcise your hearts and the hearts of your children, so that you will love *ADONAI* your God with all your heart and all your being, and thus you will live.

ISAIAH 11:11–12. On that day ADONAI will raise his hand again, a second time, to reclaim the remnant of his people who remain from Ashur, Egypt, Patros, Ethiopia, 'Eilam, Shin'ar, Hamat and the islands in the sea. He will hoist a banner for the Goyim, assemble the dispersed of Isra'el, and gather the scattered of Y'hudah from the four corners of the earth.

ISAIAH 51:11. Those ransomed by ADONAI will return and come with singing to Tziyon; on their heads will be everlasting joy. They will acquire gladness and joy, while sorrow and sighing will flee.

JEREMIAH 3:14. "Return, backsliding children," says ADONAI; "for I am your master. I will take you, one from a city, two from a family, and bring you to Tziyon."

JEREMIAH 23:3–4. "I myself will gather what remains of my flock from all the countries where I have driven them and bring them back to their homes, and they will be fruitful and increase their numbers. I will appoint shepherds over them who will shepherd them; then they will no longer be afraid or disgraced; and none will be missing," says ADONAI.

JEREMIAH 23:7–8. "Therefore," says ADONAI, "the day will come when people no longer swear, 'As ADONAI lives, who brought the people of Isra'el out of the land of Egypt,' but, 'As ADONAI lives, who brought the descendants of the house of Isra'el up from the land to the north' and from all the countries where I drove them. Then they will live in their own land."

EZEKIEL 11:17. Therefore, say that Adonai ELOHIM says this: "I will gather you from the peoples and collect you from the countries where you have been scattered, and I will give the land of Isra'el to you."

EZEKIEL 36:24. For I will take you from among the nations, gather you from all the countries, and return you to your own soil.

EZEKIEL 37:12–14. Therefore prophesy; say to them that ADONAI ELOHIM says, "My people! I will open your graves and make you get up out of your graves, and I will bring you into the land of Isra'el. Then you will know that I am ADONAI - when I have opened your graves and made you get up out of your graves, my people! I will put my Spirit in you; and you will be alive. Then I will place you in your own land; and you will know that I, ADONAI, have spoken, and that I have done it," says ADONAI.

ZECHARIAH 8:7–8. ADONAI-*Tzva'ot* says, "I will save my people from lands east and west; I will bring them back, and they will live in Yerushalayim. They will be my people; and I will be their God, with faithfulness and justice."

ZECHARIAH 10:8–12. "I will whistle for them and gather them, because I have redeemed them; they will be as numerous as they were before; and I will sow them among the peoples. In distant lands they will remember me; they will rear their children and then return. I will bring them back from the land of Egypt and gather them out of Ashur. I will bring them into Gil'ad and the L'vanon, until there is no more room for them. Trouble will pass over the sea and stir up waves in the sea; all the depths of the Nile will be dried up, the pride of Ashur will be brought down, and the scepter of Egypt will leave. But I will strengthen [Isra'el] in ADONAI; they will travel here and there in his name," says ADONAI.

Armageddon

JOEL 3:2–3. I will gather all nations and bring them down to the Valley of Y'hoshafat [ADONAI judges]. I will enter into judgment there for my people, my heritage Isra'el, whom they scattered among the nations; then they divided my land. They drew lots for my people, traded boys for whores, sold girls for wine to drink.

JOEL 3:11–16. "Hurry, come, you surrounding nations, gather yourselves together!" Bring your warriors down, ADONAI! "Let the nations be roused and come up to the Valley of Y'hoshafat [ADONAI judges]. For there I will sit to judge all the surrounding nations." Swing the sickle, for the harvest is ripe; come, and tread, for the winepress is full. The vats are overflowing, for their wickedness is great. Such enormous crowds in the Valley of Decision! For the Day of ADONAI is upon us in the Valley of Decision! The sun and moon have grown black, and the stars have stopped shining. ADONAI will roar from Tziyon, he will thunder from Yerushalayim, the sky and the earth will shake. But ADONAI will be a refuge for his people, a stronghold for the people of Isra'el.

ZECHARIAH 14:1–4. Look, a day is coming for ADONAI when your plunder, [Yerushalayim], will be divided right there within you. "For I will gather all the nations against Yerushalayim for war. The city will be taken, the houses will be rifled, the women will be raped, and half the city will go into exile; but the rest of the people will not be cut off from the city." Then ADONAI will go out and fight against those nations, fighting as on a day of battle. On that day his feet will stand on the Mount of Olives, which lies to the east of Yerushalayim; and the Mount of Olives will be split in half from east to west, to make a huge valley. Half of the mountain will move toward the north, and half of it toward the south.

The Restoration of Israel

ISAIAH 4:2–6. On that day, ADONAI's plant will be beautiful and glorious; and the fruit of the land will be the pride and splendor of Isra'el's survivors. Those left in Tziyon and remaining in Yerushalayim will be called holy, and everyone in Yerushalayim written down for life. When ADONAI washes away the filth of the women of Tziyon and cleanses Yerushalayim from the blood shed in it with a blast of searing judgment, ADONAI will create over the whole site of Mount Tziyon and over those who assemble there a smoking cloud by day and a shining, flaming fire by night; for the Glory will be over everything like a hupah. A sukkah will give shade by day from the heat; it will also provide refuge and cover from storm and rain.

ISAIAH 35:1–2. The desert and the dry land will be glad; the Aravah will rejoice and blossom like the lily. It will burst into flower, will rejoice with joy and singing, will be given the glory of the L'vanon, the splendor of Karmel and the Sharon. They will see the glory of ADONAI, the splendor of our God.

ISAIAH 60:1–3. Arise, shine [Yerushalayim], for your light has come, the glory of ADONAI has risen over you. For although darkness covers the earth and thick darkness the peoples; on you ADONAI will rise;

over you will be seen his glory. Nations will go toward your light and kings toward your shining splendor.

ISAIAH 61:4–7. They will rebuild the ancient ruins, restore sites long destroyed; they will renew the ruined cities, destroyed many generations ago. Strangers will stand and feed your flocks, foreigners plow your land and tend your vines; but you will be called cohanim of ADONAI, spoken of as ministers to our God. You will feed on the wealth of nations, and revel in their riches. Because of your shame, which was doubled, and because they cried, "They deserve disgrace," therefore in their land what they own will be doubled, and joy forever will be theirs.

ISAIAH 62:1–4. For Tziyon's sake I will not be silent, for Yerushalayim's sake I will not rest, until her vindication shines out brightly and her salvation like a blazing torch. The nations will see your vindication and all kings your glory. Then you will be called by a new name which ADONAI himself will pronounce. You will be a glorious crown in the hand of ADONAI, a royal diadem held by your God. You will no longer be spoken of as Azuvah [Abandoned] or your land be spoken of as Sh'mamah [Desolate]; rather, you will be called Heftzi-Vah [My-Delight-Is-In-Her] and your land Be'ulah [Married]. For ADONAI delights in you, and your land will be married.

JEREMIAH 31:31–34. "Here, the days are coming," says ADONAI, "when I will make a new covenant with the house of Isra'el and with the house of Y'hudah. It will not be like the covenant I made with their fathers on the day I took them by their hand and brought them out of the land of Egypt; because they, for their part, violated my covenant, even though I, for my part, was a husband to them," says ADONAI. "For this is the covenant I will make with the house of Isra'el after those days," says ADONAI: "I will put my Torah within them and write it on their hearts; I will be their God, and they will be my people. No longer will any of them teach his fellow community member or his brother, 'Know ADONAI'; for all will know me, from the least of them to the greatest; because I will forgive their wickednesses and remember their sins no more."

JEREMIAH 33:10–11. Here is what ADONAI says: "You say that this place is a wasteland, with neither people nor animals in the cities of Y'hudah, and that the streets of Yerushalayim are desolate, without people or animals—no inhabitants. Yet there will again be heard here the sounds of joy and gladness and the voices of bridegroom and bride, the voices of those who sing, 'Give thanks to ADONAI-Tzva'ot, for ADONAI is good, for his grace continues forever,' as they bring offerings of thanksgiving into the house of ADONAI. For I will cause those captured from the land to return, as before," says ADONAI.

AMOS 9:11–15. "When that day comes, I will raise up the fallen sukkah of David. I will close up its gaps, raise up its ruins and rebuild it as it used to be, so that Isra'el can possess what is left of Edom and of all the nations bearing my name," says ADONAI, who is doing this. "The days will come," says ADONAI, "when the plowman will overtake the reaper and the one treading grapes the one sowing seed. Sweet wine will drip down the mountains, and all the hills will flow with it. I will restore the fortunes of my people Isra'el; they will rebuild and inhabit the ruined cities; they will plant vineyards and drink their wine, cultivate gardens and eat their fruit. I will plant them on their own soil, no more to be uprooted from their land, which I gave them," says ADONAI your God.

HOSEA 14:7. Again they will live in his shade and raise grain; they will blossom like a vine, and its aroma will be like the wine of the L'vanon.

ROMANS 11:26–27. [A]nd that it is in this way that all Isra'el will be saved. As the Tanakh says, "Out of Tziyon will come the Redeemer; he will turn away ungodliness from Ya'akov and this will be my covenant with them ... when I take away their sins."

The Restoration and Expansion of Jerusalem

ISAIAH 2:2, MICAH 4:1. In the acharit-hayamim, the mountain of ADONAI's house will be established as the most important mountain. It will be regarded more highly than the other hills, and all the Goyim will stream there.

JEREMIAH 3:17. When that time comes, they will call Yerushalayim the throne of ADONAI. All the nations will be gathered there to the name of ADONAI, to Yerushalayim. No longer will they live according to their stubbornly evil hearts.

JEREMIAH 31:38,40. "Look, the days are coming," says ADONAI, "when the city will be rebuilt for ADONAI from the Tower of Hanan'el to the Corner Gate . . . it will never be uprooted or destroyed again."

EZEKIEL 47:7, 12. After being returned, I saw on the bank of the river a great number of trees on the one side and on the other. . . . "On both riverbanks will grow all kinds of trees for food; their leaves will not dry up, nor will their fruit fail. There will be a different kind of fruit each month, because the water flows from the sanctuary, so that this fruit will be edible, and the leaves will have healing properties."

ZECHARIAH 2:4–5. Run and tell this young man, "Yerushalayim will be inhabited without walls," because there will be so many people and animals; "for," says ADONAI, "I will be for her a wall of fire surrounding her; and I will be the glory within her."

ZECHARIAH 14:10–11. All the land will be made like the Aravah, from Geva to Rimmon in the Negev. Yerushalayim will be raised up and inhabited where she is, from Binyamin's Gate to the place where the earlier gate stood, and on to the Corner Gate, and from the Tower of Hanan'el to the king's winepresses. People will live there, the curse will be broken, and Yerushalayim will live in safety.

The Inclusion of the Nations

GENESIS 12:3. By you all the families of the earth will be blessed.

DEUTERONOMY 32:21. They aroused my jealousy with a non-god and provoked me with their vanities; I will arouse their jealousy with a non-people and provoke them with a vile nation.

PSALM 22:27. All the ends of the earth will remember and turn to ADONAI; all the clans of the nations will worship in your presence.

AMOS 9:12. [A]ll the nations bearing my name.

ISAIAH 2:2–3. [A]ll the Goyim will stream there. Many peoples will go and say, "Come, let's go up to the mountain of ADONAI, to the house of the God of Ya'akov! He will teach us about his ways, and we will walk in his paths." For out of Tziyon will go forth Torah, the word of ADONAI from Yerushalayim.

ISAIAH 49:6. It is not enough that you are merely my servant to raise up the tribes of Ya'akov and restore the offspring of Isra'el. I will also make you a light to the nations, so my salvation can spread to the ends of the earth.

ZECHARIAH 8:23. ADONAI-Tzva'ot says, "When that time comes, ten men will take hold—speaking all the languages of the nations—will grab hold of the cloak of a Jew and say, 'We want to go with you, because we have heard that God is with you.'"

The Temple in Messiah's Kingdom

ISAIAH 2:2–3, MICAH 4:1–2. In the acharit-hayamim the mountain of ADONAI's house will be established as the most important mountain. It will be regarded more highly than the other hills, and all the Goyim will stream there. Many peoples will go and say, "Come, let's go up to the mountain of ADONAI, to the house of the God of Ya'akov! He will teach us about his ways, and we will walk in his paths." For out of Tziyon will go forth Torah, the word of ADONAI from Yerushalayim.

ISAIAH 56:6–7. And the foreigners who join themselves to ADONAI to serve him, to love the name of ADONAI, and to be his workers, all who keep Shabbat and do not profane it, and hold fast to my covenant, I will bring them to my holy mountain and make them joyful in my house of prayer; their burnt offerings and sacrifices will be accepted on my altar; for my house will be called a house of prayer for all peoples.

ISAIAH 60:13–14. The glory of the L'vanon will come to you, cypresses together with elm trees and larches, to beautify the site of my sanctuary—I will glorify the place where I stand. The children of your oppressors will come and bow low before you, all who despised you will fall at your feet, calling you the city of ADONAI, Tziyon of the Holy One of Isra'el.

ISAIAH 66:20–21. "[A]nd they will bring all your kinsmen out of all the nations as an offering to ADONAI—on horses, in chariots, in wagons, on mules, on camels—to my holy mountain Yerushalayim," says ADONAI, "just as the people of Isra'el themselves bring their offerings in clean vessels to the house of ADONAI I will also take cohanim and L'vi'im from them," says ADONAI.

EZEKIEL 40–48. [The detailed plans for Messiah's temple, the holy days and sacrifices, the changes in the Torah, and the layout of the tribes and the land.]

HAGGAI 2:6–9. For this is what ADONAI-Tzva'ot says: "It won't be long before one more time I will shake the heavens and the earth, the sea and the dry land; and I will shake all the nations, so that the treasures of all the nations will flow in; and I will fill this house with glory," says ADONAI-Tzva'ot. "The silver is mine, and the gold is mine," says ADONAI-Tzva'ot. "The glory of this new house will surpass that of the old," says ADONAI-Tzva'ot, "and in this place I will grant shalom," says ADONAI-Tzva'ot.

MATTHEW 24:15–21. So when you see the abomination that causes devastation spoken about through the prophet Dani'el standing in the Holy Place (let the reader understand the allusion), that will be the time for those in Y'hudah to escape to the hills. If someone is on the roof, he must not go down to gather his belongings from his house; if someone is in the field, he must not turn back to get his coat. What a terrible time it will be for pregnant women and nursing mothers! Pray that you will not have to escape in winter or on Shabbat. For there will be trouble then worse than there has ever been from the beginning of the world until now, and there will be nothing like it again!

2 THESSALONIANS 2:3–4. Don't let anyone deceive you in any way. For the Day will not come until after the Apostasy has come and the man who separates himself from Torah has been revealed, the one destined for doom. He will oppose himself to everything that people call a god or make an object of worship; he will put himself above them all, so that he will sit in the Temple of God and proclaim that he himself is God.

The Torah in Messiah's Kingdom

DEUTERONOMY 30:6. Then ADONAI your God will circumcise your hearts and the hearts of your children, so that you will love ADONAI your God with all your heart and all your being, and thus you will live.

ISAIAH 56:6–7. And the foreigners who join themselves to ADONAI to serve him, to love the name of ADONAI, and to be his workers, all who keep Shabbat and do not profane it, and hold fast to my covenant, I will bring them to my holy mountain and make them joyful in my house of prayer; their burnt offerings and sacrifices will be accepted on my altar; for my house will be called a house of prayer for all peoples.

JEREMIAH 31:33. "For this is the covenant I will make with the house of Isra'el after those days," says ADONAI: "I will put my Torah within them and write it on their hearts; I will be their God, and they will be my people."

EZEKIEL 11:19–20. [A]nd I will give them unity of heart. I will put a new spirit among you. I will remove from their bodies the hearts of stone and give them hearts of flesh; so that they will live by my regulations, obey my rulings and act by them. Then they will be my people, and I will be their God.

EZEKIEL 36:27. I will put my Spirit inside you and cause you to live by my laws, respect my rulings and obey them.

God Dwelling with Men

ISAIAH 24:23. Then the moon will be confused and the sun ashamed, for *Adonai-Tzva'ot* will rule on Mount Tziyon and in Yerushalayim, with his glory manifest to the rulers of his people.

JEREMIAH 3:17. When that time comes, they will call Yerushalayim the throne of *Adonai*, All the nations will be gathered there to the name of *Adonai*, to Yerushalayim. No longer will they live according to their stubbornly evil hearts.

EZEKIEL 37:26–28. I will make a covenant of peace with them, an everlasting covenant. I will give to them, increase their numbers, and set my sanctuary among them forever. My home will be with them; I will be their God, and they will be my people. The nations will know that I am *Adonai*, who sets Isra'el apart as holy, when my sanctuary is with them forever.

EZEKIEL 43:7. He said, "Human being, this is the place for my throne, the place for the soles of my feet, where I will live among the people of Isra'el forever. The house of Isra'el, both they and their kings, will never again defile my holy name..."

EZEKIEL 48:35. The perimeter of [the city] will be just under six [miles] long. And from that day on the name of the city will be *Adonai* Shamah [*Adonai* is there].

MICAH 4:6–7. "When that day comes," says *Adonai*, "I will assemble the lame and gather those who were dispersed, along with those I afflicted. I will make the lame a remnant and those who were driven off a strong nation." *Adonai* will rule them on Mount Tziyon from that time forth and forever.

2 CORINTHIANS 6:16. I will house myself in them ... and I will walk among you. I will be their God, and they will be my people.

REVELATION 21:3–4. See! God's Sh'khinah is with mankind, and he will live with them. They will be his people, and he himself, God-with-them, will be their God. He will wipe away every tear from their eyes. There will no longer be any death; and there will no longer be any mourning, crying or pain; because the old order has passed away.

REVELATION 22:5. Night will no longer exist, so they will need neither the light of a lamp nor the light of the sun, because ADONAI, God, will shine upon them.

Agricultural Paradise

ISAIAH 25:6. On this mountain ADONAI-Tzva'ot will make for all peoples a feast of rich food and superb wines, delicious, rich food and superb, elegant wines.

JOEL 3:18. Then, when that time comes, the mountains will drip with sweet wine, the hills will flow with milk, all the streambeds of Y'hudah will run with water, and a spring will flow from the house of ADONAI to water the Sheetim Valley.

AMOS 9:13–14. "The days will come," says ADONAI, "when the plowman will overtake the reaper and the one treading grapes the one sowing seed. Sweet wine will drip down the mountains, and all the hills will flow with it. I will restore the fortunes of my people Isra'el; they will rebuild and inhabit the ruined cities; they will plant vineyards and drink their wine, cultivate gardens and eat their fruit."

MICAH 4:4. Instead, each person will sit under his vine and fig tree, with no one to upset him, for the mouth of ADONAI-Tzva'ot has spoken.

ZECHARIAH 3:10. "When that time comes," says ADONAI-Tzva'ot, "you will all invite each other to join you under your vines and fig trees."

The Coming of Messiah

GENESIS 22:18. [A]nd by your descendants all the nations of the earth will be blessed - because you obeyed my order.

GENESIS 49:10. The scepter will not pass from Y'hudah, nor the ruler's staff from between his legs, until he comes to whom [obedience] belongs; and it is he whom the peoples will obey.

Note: "until he comes to whom [obedience] belongs," or "until Shiloh comes," or "until tribute comes to him."

NUMBERS 24:17. I see him, but not now; I behold him, but not soon —a star will step forth from Ya'akov, a scepter will arise from Isra'el, to crush the corners of Mo'av and destroy all descendants of Shet.

ISAIAH 9:6–7. For a child is born to us, a son is given to us; dominion will rest on his shoulders, and he will be given the name Pele-Yo'etz El Gibbor Avi-'Ad Sar-Shalom [Wonder of a Counselor, Mighty God, Father of Eternity, Prince of Peace], in order to extend the dominion and perpetuate the peace of the throne and kingdom of David, to secure it and sustain it through justice and righteousness henceforth and forever. The zeal of ADONAI-*Tzva'ot* will accomplish this.

ISAIAH 11:1–5. But a branch will emerge from the trunk of Yishai, a shoot will grow from his roots. The Spirit of ADONAI will rest on him, the Spirit of wisdom and understanding, the Spirit of counsel and power, the Spirit of knowledge and fearing ADONAI—he will be inspired by fearing ADONAI. He will not judge by what his eyes see or decide by what his ears hear, but he will judge the impoverished justly; he will decide fairly for the humble of the land. He will strike the land with a rod from his mouth and slay the wicked with a breath from his lips. Justice will be the belt around his waist, faithfulness the sash around his hips.

ISAIAH 61:1–4. The Spirit of *Adonai* ELOHIM is upon me, because ADONAI has anointed me to announce good news to the poor. He has sent me to heal the brokenhearted; to proclaim freedom to the captives, to let out into light those bound in the dark; to proclaim the year of the favor of ADONAI and the day of vengeance of our God; to comfort all who mourn, yes, provide for those in Tziyon who mourn, giving them garlands instead of ashes, the oil of gladness instead of mourning, a cloak of praise instead of a heavy spirit, so that they will be called oaks of righteousness planted by ADONAI, in which he takes pride. They will rebuild the ancient ruins, restore sites long destroyed; they will renew the ruined cities, destroyed many generations ago.

JEREMIAH 23:5–6. "The days are coming," says ADONAI, "when I will raise a righteous Branch for David. He will reign as king and succeed, he will do what is just and right in the land. In his days Y'hudah will be saved, Isra'el will live in safety, and the name given to him will be ADONAI Tzidkenu [ADONAI our righteousness]."

JEREMIAH 30:21–22. "Their leader will be one of their own, their ruler will come from among them. I will cause him to come close and let him approach me; for, otherwise, who would guarantee his heart enough to approach me?" says ADONAI. "You will be my people, and I will be your God."

JEREMIAH 33:15. When those days come, at that time, I will cause to spring up for David a Branch of Righteousness. He will do what is just and right in the land.

EZEKIEL 21:27. Ruin! Ruin! I will leave it a ruin such as there has never been, and it will stay that way until the rightful ruler comes, and I give it to him.

EZEKIEL 34:23–24. I will raise up one shepherd to be in charge of them, and he will let them feed—my servant David. He will pasture them and be their shepherd. I, ADONAI, will be their God; and my servant David will be prince among them. I, ADONAI, have spoken.

EZEKIEL 37:24. My servant David will be king over them, and all of them will have one shepherd; they will live by my rulings and keep and observe my regulations.

DANIEL 7:13–14. I kept watching the night visions, when I saw, coming with the clouds of heaven, someone like a son of man. He approached the Ancient One and was led into his presence. To him was given rulership, glory and a kingdom, so that all peoples, nations and languages should serve him. His rulership is an eternal rulership that will not pass away; and his kingdom is one that will never be destroyed.

HOSEA 3:5. Afterwards, the people of Isra'el will repent and seek ADONAI their God and David their king; they will come trembling to ADONAI and his goodness in the acharit-hayamim.

MICAH 5:2. But you, Beit-Lechem near Efrat, so small among the clans of Y'hudah, out of you will come forth to me the future ruler of Isra'el, whose origins are far in the past, back in ancient times.

ZECHARIAH 9:9–10. Rejoice with all your heart, daughter of Tziyon! Shout out loud, daughter of Yerushalayim! Look! Your king is coming to you. He is righteous, and he is victorious. Yet he is humble—he's riding on a donkey, yes, on a lowly donkey's colt. I will banish chariots from Efrayim and war-horses from Yerushalayim." The warrior's bow will be banished, and he will proclaim peace to the nations. He will rule from sea to sea, and from the [Euphrates] River to the ends of the earth.

ALSO, THE SUFFERING MESSIAH: Isaiah 42:1-4; 49:1–7; 50:4-9; 52:13–53:12; Daniel 9:25-26; Zechariah 12:10.

Ages Past and To Come

Eden

... on the day that you eat from it, it will become certain that you will die....
Genesis 2:17

Eden was not the perfect paradise, not yet. God made man and woman innocent. He had a plan to teach them more, good and evil, the meaning of free will and righteousness. Eden was a paradise waiting to happen if man and woman would love God in spite of the choice to do otherwise. There was no death. There was not yet any evil there. But evil had been introduced already among the sons of God, the heavenly beings. And one, in the form of a serpent, brought that evil into the almost-paradise and it wasn't. Men and women have been living in exile ever since. But the memory of paradise lives on and draws us on.

The Nations Before Abraham

Look, the people are united, they all have a single language, and see what they're starting to do! At this rate, nothing they set out to accomplish will be impossible for them! Come, let's go down and confuse their language, so that they won't understand each other's speech... Genesis 11:6-7

Depravity and mob mentality spread quickly in this period. God was bothered most by the violence and sent the flood to slow the spread of evil. General revelations to the nations did not bring people to trust in God. They began to make gods in their image rather than honor the God who made them in his.

Patriarchal Days

... by you all the families of the earth will be blessed. Genesis 12:3

God chose one man. He made a plan that was fool-proof because it depended only on divine providence. All Abraham's descendants had to do was be born. God would bless the nations through his offspring. Faith was not a prerequisite and neither was obedience. The existence of the Jewish people, the children of Jacob, is all God needs to redeem and perfect this world. From Jacob on the world became divided into Israel and the nations and God's plan always comes through Israel to bless the nations.

Torah and the Land

... and you shall be to me a kingdom of priests and a holy nation. Exodus 19:6 (ESV)

The children of Jacob received the Torah, the revelation of who God is and what he expects of his people. They soon after received the land, the place from which all of God's great plans for redeeming and perfecting the world would take place. A holy book and a holy land were given to a holy people. Yet even if Israel was not obedient, God's work through them was destined to succeed. They were to be priests, willing or not, and the world has been changed by the children of Jacob. From the calendar to the world's outlook on religion, nothing has been the same since.

Exile

By the rivers of Bavel we sat down and wept as we remembered Tziyon. Psalm 137:1

Jerusalem, like Eden, was now a place cut off from them. They prayed they would never forget the dream that had been Jerusalem, Zion the city of God. The ark and the glory were gone. The holy people were captives now in the nations. When it was at last time to return, relatively few came. The second Temple was not so glorious. But among those exiles and returnees hope began to grow. Pious ones and seers taught of a coming time of righteousness, cataclysm, and Messiah. Angels and visions of the end were growing in the people's imagination. They were a people waiting for Messiah.

Messiah's Appearance

They took palm branches and went out to meet him, shouting, "Deliver us!" "Blessed is he who comes in the name of ADONAI, the King of Isra'el!"
John 12:13

He came in a way that was far less dramatic than many had hoped. He subverted their ideas about the kingdom of God, the coming Messianic Age. He did not put away Rome, but called Israel to return instead to the Father. He seemed an ordinary man, or at least far more ordinary than they had imagined. What good were miracles and healings when the people wanted glory and to put away the great oppressor that was Rome. Thousands welcomed him as Israel's king, but the nation as a whole saw only a strange martyr.

Times of the Gentiles

. . . a partial hardening has come upon Israel, until the fullness of the Gentiles has come in. Romans 11:25 (ESV)

All Israel will be saved, but this is the time of the nations. From Jerusalem the word went out and men and women from all over the empire turned to Israel's God and Israel's unclaimed Messiah. Very quickly Israel was forgotten. In a short time, many even denied that God still worked through the children of Jacob. It has been an era of great glory and also of great tragedy. Men have loved the Jewish Messiah while rejecting the Jewish people. And the hearts of Israel have grown harder. But the times of the Gentiles are closing and the days of Israel are coming.

Regathering

For I will take you from among the nations, gather you from all the countries, and return you to your own soil. Ezekiel 36:24

All through history, a few faithful Jews had made the land their dream. In the late 19th and early 20th centuries they trickled in. They drained swamps. They reclaimed unwanted land within the borders of God's promise. Against all odds, and only after a near genocide, they reclaimed the land in 1948 and Jerusalem in 1967. And still they are being gathered, as only one third are now there. Few of the promises of restoration have yet come to pass. Yet many dare to dream. Visionaries. Some are preparing the third Temple. Others pray for the peace of Jerusalem. We can feel the winds of Messiah.

Messianic Woes

Its end shall come with a flood, and to the end there shall be war. Desolations are decreed. Daniel 9:26 (ESV)

Trumpets will blow. Bowls will be poured out. People will ask mountains to fall on them and cover them from God's anger. Even Jerusalem will be overrun by the end. The holy city will be attacked. All nations will join in a battle at a place called Armageddon. Israel will turn to Messiah, starting with a group called the 144,000. These are pious young men who will lead their nation to Messiah. After great pain, he will stand on the Mount of Olives and rescue his people. Redemption and perfection are now near.

Days of Messiah

Blessed and holy is anyone who has a part in the first resurrection; over him the second death has no power. On the contrary, they will be cohanim of God and of the Messiah, and they will rule with him for the thousand years. Revelation 20:6

The Holy One, the King, will take his throne in Jerusalem. A river of life will flow from the Temple there and trees with healing leaves will grow on its banks. The faithful from all the previous eras will be here, resurrected and never to die again. Even those born in this time will live long lives, with one hundred being a young age to die. The hills will be covered with vineyards and every person will sit under his own vine and fig tree. The nations will all come, year after year at Sukkot, to worship Messiah Yeshua at his Jerusalem Temple. And Jerusalem will be called "Adonai is our righteousness."

Final Age

Also I saw the holy city, New Yerushalayim, coming down out of heaven from God, prepared like a bride beautifully dressed for her husband. Revelation 21:2

The last deception will be at the end of the days of Messiah and Satan will lead many astray. But after his rebellion is put away, all sin and death will cease. The faithful will enter into the magic hills and go beyond the joys even of the days of Messiah. It will be a New Earth and a New Jerusalem, like the best things of the old, only better. Everything good in this life will be better in the World to Come. Everything bad will be gone forever. And there will be no sun or moon, for Adonai will be our light.

ENDNOTES

Chapter One

1. Mishnah, Sanhedrin 10:1.
2. Asimov as cited in Joey Green, *Philosophy on the Go* (Running Press, 2007), p. 222.
3. 1 Corinthians 2:9 (quoting Isaiah 64:4).
4. Randy Alcorn, *Heaven* (Carol Stream: Tyndale, 2004), pp. 18–19.
5. Hebrews 11:10.
6. A.J. Conyers, *The Eclipse of Heaven* (Downer's Grove: InterVarsity Press, 1992), p. 21.
7. N.T. Wright, *The Resurrection of the Son of God* (Minneapolis: Fortress, 2003), p. 39.
8. Piotr Beinkowski and Alan Millard, *Dictionary of the Ancient Near East* (Philadelphia: Univ. of Pennsylvania Press, 2000), p. 88.
9. Henri Frankfort, *Ancient Egyptian Religion* (New York: Harper and Row, 1948), pp. 88–123.
10. Wright, p. 40.
11. Ibid., p. 52.
12. Ibid., p. 50.
13. Ibid., p. 78.
14. Proverbs 10:24 and 11:23 (ESV).
15. Jeremiah 50:19 (ESV).
16. Psalm 37:4 (ESV).

Chapter Two

1. Abraham is called a prophet in Genesis 20:7, but this is only in a limited sense.
2. Isaiah 1:7.
3. Deuteronomy 30:1 (ESV).
4. Deuteronomy 30:1–6.
5. Jeremiah 31:31–34; Ezekiel 36:24–32.
6. Ecclesiastes 9:11 (ESV).
7. Isaiah 22:13.
8. Job 7:6.
9. Amos 1:1.

10. Amos 9:11.

11. Note how James used this very passage in Acts 15:16–17 as
     God's authorization for including Gentiles in the congregations
     of Messiah.

12. Babylonian Talmud, Kethubot 111b.

13. Jerusalem Talmud, Taanit 64a.

14. Mark 13:2.

15. Isaiah 2:2–3 (ESV, the Lord changed to Adonai).

16. Paul also envisions the Temple existing in the last days (2
     Thess. 2:4). The place of the Temple and the sacrifices in the
     World to Come are difficult for many to understand because
     for too long Christians have interpreted the cross of Jesus
     as a replacement of the Temple sacrifices. The true purpose
     of the Temple sacrifices is obscured by centuries of neglect
     of Leviticus. It is better to say that the Temple sacrifices
     pointed to the need for a greater kind of atonement than
     these sacrifices could provide. The Temple sacrifices did not
     cleanse the person, but cleansed the Temple of the person's
     sins and impurities. It wasn't until the cross that purification
     for a person's being was available. For more see my book *A
     New Look at the Old Testament* and the chapter "Bulls, Goats,
     and Worship."

17. Jeremiah 31:33.

18. Ezekiel 36:27.

19. Ezekiel 40–48.

20. See note 16 from this chapter about the Temple in the World
     to Come.

21. The origins of the term *Tikkun Olam* are in Lurianic kabbalah.
     I am not using the expression in the kabbalistic sense, but in
     the broader sense commonly used in contemporary Judaism.
     The world is broken and God expects us to work with him in
     repairing it.

22. See chapter 5, "Yeshua and the Kingdom of God," for Yeshua's
     instruction to us to be involved in Tikkun Olam.

23. Norman Snaith, *The Distinctive Ideas of the Old Testament* (New
     York: Schocken, 1964), p. 73.

24. Amos 2:6–7.

25. Amos 5:23–24.

26. Isaiah 58:6–7.

27. Hosea 6:6.
28. Micah 6:8.
29. Micah 4:4 (ESV).
30. C.S. Lewis, *The Great Divorce* (New York: MacMillan Publishing Company, 1946).
31. Genesis 2:9.

Chapter Three

1. Michael Wyschograd, *Body of Faith* (Northvale: Aronson, 1996), pp. 175-177.
2. R. Kendall Soulen, *The God of Israel and Christian Theology* (Minneapolis: Fortress, 1996), pp. 25-27.
3. Ibid.
4. This point was brought home to me by Rabbi Dr. Mark Kinzer in a course I took from him on Messianic Jewish Theology. I doubted the point at first, but when I saw it in Genesis, it opened up my imagination and my understanding.
5. cf. Deuteronomy 4:25-31, 30:1-6, and 32:1-43.
6. Jeremiah 31:31 (ESV).
7. Romans 11:2, 28 (ESV).
8. Zechariah 14:3-4.
9. Deuteronomy 30:3-4.
10. Zechariah 14:2 (ESV).
11. Joel 3:2 (ESV). See also vv. 9-16.
12. Joel 3:13.
13. Matthew 23:39.
14. Ezekiel 47:13.
15. Isaiah 2:2 (ESV, the Lord changed to Adonai).
16. Isaiah 2:3 (ESV, the Lord changed to Adonai).
17. Zechariah 8:23.
18. Isaiah 19:24-25 (ESV, the Lord changed to Adonai).
19. Ezekiel 36:26-27. See also Deuteronomy 30:6 and Jeremiah 31:33.
20. Ezekiel 47:12.
21. Isaiah 9:7 (ESV).
22. Jeremiah 33:18 (ESV). See also Ezekiel 43.
23. Ezekiel 43:7 (ESV).
24. Jeremiah 29:11.

Chapter Four

1. Psalm 8:4-5 (ESV).
2. Genesis 2:7.
3. Rob Bell, *Sex God* (Grand Rapids: Zondervan, 2007), p. 50.
4. Jeremiah 31:3.
5. Hosea 11:8-9 (ESV).
6. Genesis 12:2.
7. Genesis 12:3 (ESV). There is some debate about whether the verb is passive (be blessed) or reflexive (bless themselves). Since Gen. 22:18 uses the reflexive (hitpa'el form), I presume that the ambiguous form in 12:3 (niphal) is passive.
8. Genesis 12:3.
9. Genesis 20.
10. Genesis 26:6-31.
11. cf. Genesis 37-50. Soulen uses this illustration as a paradigm for the blessing pattern God intended: the nations are blessed through Israel. *The God of Israel and Christian Theology*, pp. 128-129.
12. Deuteronomy 32:21 (ESV).
13. The texts on the sojourner are numerous, but Numbers 15:14-16 is a good summary. Exodus 12:48 shows one limitation: the sojourner may not eat the Passover sacrifice unless he is circumcised.
14. 1 Kings 8:41-43.
15. Psalm 22:27-28.
16. Psalm 67:4-7.
17. Psalm 72:17 (ESV), see also Psalm 86:9; 96:7; 98:2-4; 99:3; and 117:1.
18. Amos 9:12 (ESV). James quotes this verse in Acts 15:16-17 as proof that Gentiles need not convert. The key phrase is "Gentiles who are called by my name," i.e., they do not need to become Jews.
19. Isaiah 2:2-3 (ESV, the Lord changed to Adonai).
20. Isaiah 42:6-7 (ESV).
21. Isaiah 49:6 (ESV).
22. Isaiah 60:3. See also Ezekiel 37:28.
23. Isaiah 66:19-21 (ESV, the Lord changed to Adonai).
24. Joel 3:2 (ESV).

25. Zechariah 8:23.
26. Zechariah 14:16 (ESV, the Lord changed to Adonai).
27. Zechariah 14:9.

Chapter Five

1. Mark 4:30-32.
2. A leading theory about the pseudepigraphical Psalms of Solomon is that a group such as the Pharisees write them shortly after Pompei desecrated the Temple in 63 B.C.E. They speak of a warrior Messiah who will expel the Kittim, a code name for the Romans.
3. Zechariah 14:3.
4. Numbers 24:17-18 (ESV).
5. N.T. Wright, *The New Testament and the People of God* (Minneapolis: Fortress, 1992), p. 303.
6. Ibid., p. 304.
7. N.T. Wright, *Jesus and the Victory of God* (Minneapolis: Fortress, 1996), p. 199.
8. Ibid., p. 199.
9. Ibid., p. 199.
10. John 18:34, 36 (ESV).
11. Luke 6:29.
12. Matthew 3:2 (ESV).
13. Matthew 8:11-12 (ESV).
14. Matthew 11:12 (ESV).
15. Matthew 18:3.
16. Matthew 5:9.
17. Matthew 22:30.
18. Matthew 5:3-10.
19. Mark 1:15.
20. Wright, *The New Testament and the People of God*, p. 194.
21. Matthew 7:21 (ESV).
22. Matthew 5:3-11.
23. Luke 16:19-31.
24. Matthew 19:30.
25. Matthew 8:11-12.
26. Matthew 7:23 (ESV).
27. Matthew 25:31-46.

28. Proverbs 19:17.
29. Matthew 18:2-4.
30. John 12:46.

Chapter Six

1. In spite of many arguments to the contrary, I am working with the view that John, one of the twelve disciples, is the John of Revelation.
2. I John 2:15.
3. For extensive documentation on Gentile God-fearers in the synagogues see Louis Feldman, *Jew and Gentile in the Ancient World* (Princeton: Princeton Univ. Press, 1993).
4. Mark Nanos, *The Irony of Galatians* (Minneapolis: Fortress, 2002), p. 258.
5. The theories about Revelation's setting and occasion are varied. A common reading places Revelation during the reign of Domitian and assumes some type of persecution, either local outbreaks or empire-wide policies.
6. Revelation 12:6 and 14.
7. Revelation 11:2.
8. Exodus 25:9, 40.
9. Hebrews 9:11.
10. Exodus 30:18.
11. Matthew 23:39.
12. Revelation 11:13.
13. Revelation 11:15.
14. Zechariah 13:9.
15. Revelation 7:9.
16. Isaiah 61:1-2.
17. Luke 4:16-22, compare Isaiah 61:1-3.
18. Isaiah 63:1-6.
19. Memra is Aramaic for *word* or *speech*. It is used in Jewish Targums much as John uses "the word" in John 1.
20. Abraham Cohen, *Everyman's Talmud* (New York: Schocken, 1949), p. 356.
21. Midrash Tanchuma Ekev, par.7, in Cohen, p. 356.
22. As often happens in prophetic passages, Revelation 20:4-6 leaves some questions unanswered. One of them is when the rest of the faithful from Israel and the nations are resurrected.

Some theorize that these will have already been raised before the tribulation or some time during. No text of the Bible confirms this theory, but neither does Revelation 20 make clear when all the faithful will be raised.

23. This is a major problem for amillennialism, the view that the thousand years is symbolic for the present age. If there is never an earthly kingdom of Messiah, then God's promises to Israel are made a mockery.

24. Revelation 21:2.

Chapter Seven

1. C. S. Lewis, *The Great Divorce* (New York: MacMillan Publishing Company, 1946), p. 122.

2. Ibid., p. 29.

3. Thanks to Curtis and Eldredge for this insight into heart-language. Brent Curtis and John Eldredge, *The Sacred Romance* (Nashville: Thomas Nelson, 1997), p. 3.

4. C. S. Lewis, *Surprised By Joy* (London: Harcourt, Brace, & Company, 1956), p. 18.

5. Isaiah 40:1 (ESV).

6. Isaiah 40:2 (ESV).

7. Isaiah 40:11 (ESV).

8. Isaiah 40:31.

9. Psalm 37:4 (ESV).

10. Ecclesiastes 3:11.

Chapter Eight

1. Revelation 20:10.

2. Matthew 25:41.

3. Lee Strobel, *The Case for Faith* (Grand Rapids: Zondervan, 2000), pp. 17-18.

4. Isaiah 66:2.

5. Isaiah 66:3-4.

6. Isaiah 66:24.

7. Mark 9:48.

8. Matthew 25:46.

9. Christopher Morgan and Robert Peterson, *Hell Under Fire* (Grand Rapids: Zondervan, 2004), p. 142.

10.   cited in *Hell Under Fire*, p. 202.
11.   C. S. Lewis, *The Great Divorce* (New York: MacMillan Publishing Company, 1946), p. 67.
12.   Bab. Talmud, Rosh HaShanah 16b. Abraham Cohen, *Everyman's Talmud* (New York: Schocken, 1949), p. 377.
13.   Ibid., p. 376.
14.   Strobel, p. 251.
15.   Ibid., pp. 245-246.
16.   Matthew 10:15 (ESV); 11:24; Luke 10:12.
17.   Matthew 23:23.
18.   *The Great Divorce*, p. 124.

Chapter Nine

1.   Abraham Cohen, *Everyman's Talmud* (New York: Schocken, 1949), p. 364.
2.   Daniel 2.
3.   Daniel 7.
4.   Daniel 2:44.
5.   Daniel 7:9-14 (ESV).
6.   Daniel 7:17 (ESV).
7.   Daniel 7:15-28.
8.   Joel 3:1-2.
9.   Joel 3:13.
10.   Zechariah 12:2.
11.   Zechariah 12:10.
12.   Zechariah 14:1-4.
13.   Zechariah 14:16-17.
14.   Zechariah 14:9, 20-21.
15.   D.A. Carson, *Matthew: Expositor's Bible Commentary*. (Grand Rapids: Zondervan, 1984).
16.   Matthew 24:3.

Chapter Ten

1.   Abraham Cohen, *Everyman's Talmud* (New York: Schocken, 1949), p. 346.
2.   Ibid., p. 346.
3.   Ibid., p. 347, Bab. Talmud Pesahim 54a.
4.   Ibid., p. 348.

5. Ibid., p. 349, Bab. Talmud Sanhedrin 98a.
6. Ibid., p. 350. Bab. Talmud Sanhedrin 97a.
7. Ibid., p. 351. Bab. Talmud Yoma 86b.
8. Ibid., p. 352. Bab. Talmud Shabbat 118b.
9. 2 Peter 3:12.
10. See Cohen, p. 356, for evidence that the rabbis saw the Days of Messiah as a transitionary stage to the World to Come.
11. Cohen, p. 352, Bab. Talmud Kethubot 111b.
12. Ibid., p. 352, Bab. Talmud Shabbat 30b.
13. Ibid., p. 353. Exodus Rabbah 15:21.
14. Rabbi Nosson Scherman, ed. *The Artscroll Siddur (Weekday Edition, Ashkenaz)* (Brooklyn: Mesorah Publications, 1988), p. 108.
15. Zechariah 14:1-4.
16. Hosea 3:5.
17. Micah 5:2-4 (5:1-3 in Jewish Bibles).
18. Isaiah 11:1.
19. Isaiah 61:3.
20. Jeremiah 33:11.
21. Matthew 10:6; Mark 15:24.
22. Matthew 23:37-39 and Luke 19:41-44. "Blessed is he who comes in the name of the Lord" is a greeting to a bridegroom at a wedding.
23. Genesis 12:3; 22:18.
24. Deuteronomy 32:21.
25. Psalm 22:27.
26. Isaiah 49:6.
27. Isaiah 2:2-3.
28. *The Artscroll Siddur,* p. 99.
29. Ibid., p. 100.
30. John 5:28-29.
31. 1 Thessalonians 4:16-17.
32. 1 Corinthians 15:52.
33. 1 Corinthians 15:36-38.
34. 1 Corinthians 15:40-41.
35. Isaiah 11:3-4.
36. Psalm 13:1-2 (2-3 in Jewish Bibles).
37. Ecclesiastes 4:1.
38. Job 21:7.
39. 2 Timothy 2:12; Revelation 20:6.

40.   Isaiah 2:4.
41.   Jeremiah 3:16.
42.   Jeremiah 3:17.
43.   I Corinthians 1:30.
44.   2 Peter 3:12.
45.   *The Artscroll Siddur*, p. 53.
46.   Titus 2:11-13.

Chapter Eleven

1.   Robert Bridges, "My Delight and They Delight," in Geoffrey O'Brien, ed., *Bartlett's Poems For Occasions* (New York: Little, Brown, and Company: 2004), p. 317.
2.   Samuel Daniel, "Love," in Debra Star, ed., *Love Poems: Four Centuries of Great Love Poems* (Borders Classics, 2006), p. 194.
3,   Emerson, "Give All to Love," in Ibid., p. 201.
4.   Georgia Douglas Johnson, "I Want to Die While You Love Me," in O'Brian, p. 327.
5.   William Blake, "The Clod and the Pebble," in Starr, p. 193.
6.   2 Samuel 1:26.
7.   I John 4:8.
8.   Song of Solomon 8:7, RSV.
9.   Rob Bell, *Sex God* (Grand Rapids: Zondervan, 2007), p. 50.
10.   2 Peter 3:16.
11.   2 Corinthians 12:2-4.
12.   Ephesians 5:16; Colossians 4:5.

Chapter Twelve

1.   Randy Alcorn, *Heaven* (Carol Stream: Tyndale, 2004), p. 171.
2.   Ibid.
3.   Rob Bell, *Sex God* (Grand Rapids: Zondervan, 2007), pp. 166-167.
4.   Romans 1:20.
5.   Bab. Talmud, Hullin 60a, as cited in David S. Ariel, *What Do Jews Believe?* (New York: Schocken, 1995), p. 23.
6.   From *The City of God* as cited in Alcorn, p. 174.
7.   From Edwards' sermon "The Christian Pilgrim," as cited in Alcorn, p. 179.
8.   John 14:1-4.

9. John 14:20.
10. John 17:24-26.

Chapter Thirteen

1 C. S. Lewis, *The Great Divorce* (New York: MacMillan Publishing Company, 1946), p. 29.
2. Ibid., p. 72.
3. I Corinthians 13:12.
4. Matthew 6:19-20.
5. Colossians 3:2.
6. Hebrews 11:10.
7. Citation taken from the Soncino English Translation of the Babylonian Talmud.
8. John 11:25-26.
9. Matthew 10:32.
10. I Corinthians 15:43.
11. I Corinthians 15:36-38.
12. I Corinthians 15:40-44.
13. 2 Peter 3:12-13.
14. 2 Peter 3:11.
15. Lewis, from *Mere Christianity*, cited in Randy Alcorn, *Heaven* (Carol Stream: Tyndale, 2004), p. 21.
16. Alcorn, p. 18.
17. From *Pirkei Avot*, as cited in Abraham Cohen, *Everyman's Talmud* (New York: Schocken, 1949), p. 366.

BIBLIOGRAPHY

Alcorn, Randy. *Heaven.* Carol Stream: Tyndale, 2004.

Ariel, David S. *What Do Jews Believe?* New York: Schocken, 1995.

Beinkowski, Piotr and Millard, Alan. *Dictionary of the Ancient Near East.* Philadelphia: Univ. of Pennsylvania Press, 2000.

Bell, Rob. *Sex God.* Grand Rapids: Zondervan, 2007.

Carson, D.A. *Matthew: Expositor's Bible Commentary.* Grand Rapids: Zondervan, 1984.

Cohen, Abraham. *Everyman's Talmud.* New York: Schocken, 1949.

Conyers, A.J. *The Eclipse of Heaven.* Downer's Grove: InterVarsity Press, 1992.

Curtis, Brent and Eldredge, John. *The Sacred Romance.* Nashville: Thomas Nelson, 1997.

Feldman, Louis. *Jew and Gentile in the Ancient World.* Princeton: Princeton Univ. Press, 1993.

Frankfort, Henri. *Ancient Egyptian Religion.* New York: Harper and Row, 1948.

Green, Joey. *Philosophy on the Go.* Running Press, 2007.

Leman, Derek. *A New Look at the Old Testament.* Stone Mountain: Mt. Olive Press, 2006.

Lewis, C.S. *The Great Divorce.* New York: MacMillan Publishing Company, 1946.

Lewis, C.S. *Surprised By Joy.* London: Harcourt, Brace, & Company, 1956.

Morgan, Christopher and Peterson, Robert. *Hell Under Fire.* Grand Rapids: Zondervan, 2004.

Nanos, Mark. *The Irony of Galatians.* Minneapolis: Fortress, 2002.

Scherman, Rabbi Nosson ed. *The Artscroll Siddur (Weekday Edition, Ashkenaz)*. Brooklyn: Mesorah Publications, 1988.

Snaith, Norman. *The Distinctive Ideas of the Old Testament*. New York: Schocken, 1964.

Soulen, R. Kendall. *The God of Israel and Christian Theology*. Minneapolis: Fortress, 1996.

Strobel, Lee. *The Case for Faith*. Grand Rapids: Zondervan, 2000.

Wright, N.T. *The New Testament and the People of God*. Minneapolis: Fortress, 1992.

Wright, N.T. *Jesus and the Victory of God*. Minneapolis: Fortress, 1996.

Wright, N.T. *The Resurrection of the Son of God*. Minneapolis: Fortress, 2003.

Wyschograd, Michael. *Body of Faith*. Northvale: Aronson, 1996.

Complete Jewish Bible

Presenting the Word of God as a unified Jewish book, here is an English translation for Jews and non-Jews alike. Names and key terms are presented in easy-to-understand transliterated Hebrew, enabling the reader to pronounce them the way Yeshua (Jesus) did!

Available in Hardback, Paperback, Blue Bonded Leather and Large Print (hardback)

God's Appointed Times

A Practical Guide for Understanding and Celebrating the Biblical Holidays
How can the biblical holy days such as Passover/ Unleavened Bread and Tabernacles be observed? What do they mean for Christians today? This book provides an easily understandable and hands-on approach. Discusses historical background, traditional Jewish observance, New Testament relevance, and prophetic significance.

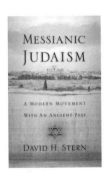

Messianic Judaism

A Modern Movement with an Ancient Past
In the first century, tens of thousands of Jewish people followed Yeshua (Jesus), believing him to be the promised Messiah of Israel. They didn't renounce their heritage, their customs, nor their people. They remained Jews. Two thousand years later, hundreds of thousands of Jewish people follow Yeshua. They too have not renounced their heritage, customs nor their people.

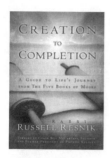

Creation to Completion
A Guide to Life's Journey from the Five Books of Moses
Have you ever wondered if the Pentateuch—the Five books of Moses—is relevant to your life? In *Creation to Completion*, Rabbi Russell Resnick offers insight into the Torah and how the commandments contribute to society today. He shows that the Creator still desires his creatures to participate in bringing the world to completion.

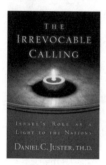

The Irrevocable Calling
Israel's Role As A Light To The Nations
Referring to the chosen-ness of the Jewish people, Paul wrote, "For God's free gifts and his calling are irrevocable" Rom. 11:29. This messenger to the Gentiles understood the unique calling of his people, Israel.

Endorsed by Jack Hayford, Don Finto and Mike Bickle, in *The Irrevocable Calling* Dr. Dan Juster expands Paul's words, showing how Israel was uniquely chosen to bless the world and how these blessings can be enjoyed today.

Proverbial Wisdom & Common Sense
A Messianic Jewish Approach to Today's Issues from the Proverbs
Unique in style and scope, this commentary on the book of Proverbs, written in devotional style, is divided into chapters suitable for daily reading. A virtual encyclopedia of practical advice from Scripture tackles vital issues, such as family relationships, sexual morality, finances, reputation and gossip, laziness and diligence—and more!

Available through **Messianic Jewish Resources International**
Visit us on the web at www.messianicjewish.net or call toll free
1-800-410-7367